Praise for
Get Out of Your Head

"This is a must-have resource for anyone looking to get control of thoughts that sometimes spin out of control. *Get Out of Your Head* is the book we all need to help us do this. It's so easy to park our minds in bad spots—to dwell on and rehash and wish things were different. But to obsess over hard things only deepens our emotional emptiness. I love how Jennie helps us see how unhealthy thoughts can be overcome by our faith, starting right now."

—LYSA TERKEURST, #1 *New York Times* best-selling author
and president of Proverbs 31 Ministries

"I know from personal experience just how easily our thoughts try to hijack our faith and throw us into a negative spiral. *Get Out of Your Head* will equip you with practical biblical tools to take control of your thoughts so they don't control you."

—CHRISTINE CAINE, best-selling author and founder of A21
and Propel Women

"My wife, Heather, and I both read this book and were deeply helped by it. *Get Out of Your Head* is packed full of truth and insight from God's Word, personal vulnerability and honesty from Jennie, and practical wisdom and encouragement for all of us. I pray and believe that God will use it to guard your heart and mind in Christ."

—DAVID PLATT, pastor of McLean Bible Church and best-selling
author of *Something Needs to Change*

"Sometimes the only barrier to our personal and spiritual growth is our thinking. Jennie Allen's new book gives us all hope and shows us how to deal with the negative thoughts that stifle and paralyze us. We need to be reminded daily of how to take every thought captive and surrender to the only One who can free us. This book is a beautiful reminder that God is at work in all the messiness of our minds. God beckons us to get out of our heads and practice daily presence and rest with Him."

—LATASHA MORRISON, author and founder of Be the Bridge

"The battle between your ears determines how you win at life. And I can testify, because of how she's personally fought for me and generations of women around the globe, there is no better faith fighter, Word warrior, and soul defender than Jennie Allen, who makes herself your personal trainer in these practical, transformational pages, alight with holy fire. She shows you how to take down anxiety, take back the mental high ground, and take more territory for the kingdom. Get out your highlighter, and get ready to gain the victory. You are about to get out of your head and get to where your heart has always hoped to be."

—ANN VOSKAMP, *New York Times* best-selling author
of *The Broken Way* and *One Thousand Gifts*

"You know those books you buy twenty copies of and then forcefully give to everyone you know? Yeah, this is one of those books. Hands down. Powerful. Prophetic. Necessary."

—JEFFERSON BETHKE, *New York Times* best-selling author
of *Jesus > Religion*

"Someone might read the title of Jennie Allen's latest book—*Get Out of Your Head: Stopping the Spiral of Toxic Thoughts*—and casually assume that it's sort of a pop-psychology 'just think positive thoughts and you'll be fine' kind of book. If so, they'd be making a wrong assumption. This substantive and probing book faithfully engages the reader with truths about the Bible, theology, science, spiritual disciplines, mental health, and, ultimately, about following Jesus. With honesty and vulnerability in sharing her own confessions and struggles, Jennie has written a book that I truly believe will challenge, bless, and empower all those who read it."

—Rev. Eugene Cho, founder of One Day's Wages and author
of *Thou Shalt Not Be a Jerk*

"Jennie Allen speaks so powerfully to this generation and teaches us so simply how to not allow our limitations to be our loudest story. Jesus > us. His desire is that we get out of our heads and live profound lives of freedom for His glory."

—Shelley Giglio, cofounder of Passion Conferences
and Passion City Church

"I'm so glad Jennie tackles a difficult topic that so many of us face. Renewing our mind is essential for a life of flourishing with God. These pages hold clear action items to help you get out of your head and on to the journey of walking free."

—Rebekah Lyons, author *Rhythms of Renewal*

"What a timely message! In *Get Out of Your Head,* my friend and mentor Jennie Allen does a beautiful job of taking your hand, leading you to those places in your mind that need healing, and allowing space for Jesus to break chains. I recommend this book to everyone—especially our generation!"

—Sadie Robertson, *New York Times* best-selling author, speaker,
and founder of Live Original

"Jennie Allen has been a trusted voice in my life for years. She is wise and kind and loves Jesus with a contagious passion rarely found. She's also fearsome in the way she loves people and engages difficult issues. You're going to find a boatload of love and truth in these pages. This book won't just change the way you think; it will alter the way you live."

—BOB GOFF, *New York Times* best-selling author of *Love Does* and *Everybody, Always*

GET OUT OF YOUR HEAD

GET OUT OF YOUR HEAD

Stopping
the Spiral
of Toxic
Thoughts

JENNIE ALLEN

Best-Selling Author of *Nothing to Prove*

WATERBROOK

Details in some anecdotes and stories have been changed to protect the identities of the persons involved.

Hardcover ISBN 978-1-60142-964-3
eBook ISBN 978-1-60142-966-7

Cover design by Mark D. Ford and Kelly L. Howard

Interior PENPAL uppercase and Penpal lowercase font design by Lauren Akers. Used by permission.

Published in association with the literary agency of Yates & Yates, www.yates2.com.

Published in the United States by WaterBrook, an imprint of Random House, a division of Penguin Random House LLC.

WATERBROOK® and its deer colophon are registered trademarks of Penguin Random House LLC.

Library of Congress Cataloging-in-Publication Data
Names: Allen, Jennie, author.
Title: Get out of your head : stopping the spiral of toxic thoughts / Jennie Allen.
Description: First Edition. | Colorado Springs : WaterBrook, 2020. | Includes bibliographical references.
Identifiers: LCCN 2019025074 | ISBN 9781601429643 (hardcover) | ISBN 9781601429667 (ebook)
Subjects: LCSH: Christian women—Religious life. | Thought and thinking—Religious aspects—Christianity.
Classification: LCC BV4527 .A448 2020 | DDC 248.4—dc23
LC record available at https://lccn.loc.gov/2019025074

Printed in the United States of America
2020—First Edition

20 19 18 17 16

SPECIAL SALES
Most WaterBrook books are available at special quantity discounts when purchased in bulk by corporations, organizations, and special-interest groups. Custom imprinting or excerpting can also be done to fit special needs. For information, please email specialmarketscms@penguinrandomhouse.com.

To the guy who always gets me out of my head.

*Zac Allen, you rescue me from myself
constantly and always point me to Jesus.
I love you and I like you.*

Be transformed by the renewal of your mind.
—ROMANS 12:2

This means it's possible.

Contents

Part Three
THINKING AS JESUS THINKS

Part One

ALL THE THOUGHTS

1

Thinking About Thinking

"TAKE EVERY THOUGHT CAPTIVE." THEY SAY AUTHORS write books for two reasons: either the author is an expert on the subject, or the subject makes the author desperate enough to spend years finding the answers. The latter most definitely describes me.

This morning I woke up intending to write to you. *But first,* I thought, *I need to spend time with God.* So what did I do? I picked up my phone. I noticed an email about something I was working on, in which the sender was "constructively" critical of my work. Just as I decided to set my phone down, something else stole my attention . . . and the next thing I knew, I was on Instagram, noticing others' wins and glories contrasted with my work in process that seemed to not be measuring up. In minutes with my phone, I decided that I was an inadequate writer, I was spending my life chasing things that mean nothing because I am nothing, I have nothing to say. I was spiraling fast into discouragement.

Then my husband, Zac, came in happy, having just met with God, and I snapped at him. My spiral began to spin faster and more chaotically. In less than an hour, I had diminished myself, criticized all my work, decided to quit ministry, ignored God, and pushed away my greatest advocate and friend.

Wow. Brilliant, Jennie. And that was only this morning? And now you want to try to help me with my chaotic thoughts?

Well, I hear you. And I imagine all my life I will be in process with this. But because of the discoveries I get to share with you here, instead of my spiral stealing a day, a week, a few years . . . just an hour into it, there was a shift in my thinking.

I did not stay paralyzed. I am free and joyful and writing to you.

I want you to know that you do not have to stay stuck either. God built a way for us to escape the downward spiral. But we rarely take it. We have bought the lie that we are victims of our thoughts rather than warriors equipped to fight on the front lines of the greatest battle of our generation: the battle for our minds.

The apostle Paul understood the war that takes place in our thoughts, how our circumstances and imaginations can become weapons that undermine our faith and hope. The Bible records his bold declaration that we are to "take every thought captive to obey Christ."[1]

Take every thought captive? Is that possible? Have you ever tried?

Once, a bird flew into our tiny house and wouldn't fly out. It took more than an hour for our whole family working together to catch that silly little sparrow. Shooting the bird with a BB gun? Easy. But capturing the wild sparrow flailing through our house was an altogether different task, a nearly impossible one.

How much more impossible to capture a wild thought on the fly? Yet the book I build my life on is telling me to capture *all my thoughts, every one of them?*

Is God serious?

Is this even possible? Because honestly my thoughts run wilder than that hyperactive sparrow.

And yours do too. I see the same wild chaos in your eyes and those of nearly every woman I meet. Like the young woman in so much pain who sat across from me this week, drowning in anxiety she has been fighting for two years. She looked at me, pleading, "Help. Tell me what to do!"

"I don't want to live anxious," she said. "I'm in counseling. I'm in Bible study. I'm willing to take medicine. I want to trust God. Why can't I change? Why do I feel so stuck in this?"

Goodness, I relate and have fought the same thing.

It's incredible, if you think about it: How can something we can't see control so much of who we are, determine what we feel and what we do and what we say or don't, dictate how we move or sleep, and inform what we want, what we hate, and what we love?

How can the thing that houses all those thoughts—just a bunch of folded tissue—contain so much of what makes us who we are?

Learning to capture our thoughts matters. **Because how we think shapes how we live.**[2]

THE PATTERNS THAT KEEP US STUCK

The subject of neuroscience has captivated me for years now, ever since one of my brilliant daughters began educating me on the science of the brain. When Kate, now a junior in high school, was in the seventh grade, she came home from school one afternoon and announced to the rest of us— her two brothers, her sister, my husband, Zac, and me—that she was going to cure Alzheimer's disease someday.

We smiled, but years later she still is reading books and articles on the subject, listening to every TED Talk on the brain, sharing research with me. Things like . . .

Did you know that more has been discovered about our minds in the last twenty years than in all the time before that?

Did you know that an estimated 60 to 80 percent of visits to primary care physicians have a stress-related component?[3]

Did you know that research shows that "75 to 98 percent of mental, physical, and behavioral illness comes from one's thought life"?[4]

Did you know that, with what we know about the brain today, when Scripture is talking about the heart, it really could be talking about the mind and the emotions we experience in our brains?

Well, no, Kate, I did not. But that's very interesting.

The truth is, it *is* very interesting to me.

Somewhere along the way, Kate's fascination became mine too. Because she taught me that what she is learning in science is also scattered throughout my Bible and many of the truths in the Bible concerning our thought lives have been backed up by science. This all became increasingly important to me as I became gripped by the idea that taking control of our minds could be the key to finding peace in the other parts of our lives.

For several years I'd been in deep running IF:Gathering, the organization I believe God prompted me to start to disciple women and equip them to go disciple others. I loved our community, our gatherings, and the impact we seemed to be having, but over time I noticed a troubling trend among the women I loved and served every day.

Women would feel conviction at an event or as they worked through our discipleship resources, and they would surrender their lives more fully to Jesus. They would soar on the wings of that resolve for a week, a month, sometimes a year or even two. But inevitably at some point they'd slip back into old habits, old patterns of doing life. Maybe you know exactly what I mean.

Maybe right now you're thinking of that toxic relationship you finally got out of but then, in a weak moment, resumed.

Or you finally found peace about a less-than-desirable season of your life—but now your emotions have spiraled downward again, and all you do is complain.

Or you were convicted about your porn habit and stopped, only to slip back into the habit weeks later.

Or you recognized a pattern of being critical of your spouse, surrendered it, and truly started to change . . . just before you circled back to where you began.

Why, I wondered, *don't the changes so many women desperately want to make stick over the long haul?*

And why did I still struggle with some of the same fears, negative patterns, and other sins that I had been fighting for years?

Even as I observed this boomerang effect at a broad level, I was also in relationship with dear friends, women I knew well, who seemed to battle the same issues year after year. Each time we'd get together, I'd hear the same song, five hundredth verse.

What prevented them from thriving? Why couldn't they get unstuck? Kate's discoveries as she continued to study the brain suggested one strong possibility:

It's all in our heads.

BREAKING THE SPIRAL

There is much we don't know about the brain. But what's also true, like Kate says: we've learned more about the brain in the past twenty years than we knew for the previous two thousand. We once thought of the mind as an immutable thing. The brain you were born with and the way it worked—or didn't—were just "how it was"; no sense fretting over what can't be changed. We now know that **the brain is constantly changing, whether or not we intend for it to.**

In hopes of discovering how women can break free from our problematic patterns, I started picking up heady books about the mind and about neuroscience and about how real change occurs. I watched TED Talks that Kate pointed me toward about our brain's plasticity.

I listened to brainy podcasts.

I watched brainy documentaries.

I talked to brainy people.

I began to see a pattern at work in many of us. Our emotions were leading us to thoughts, and those thoughts were dictating our decisions, and our decisions were determining behaviors, and then the behaviors were shaping our relationships, all of which would take us back to either healthy or unhealthy thoughts.

Round and round and round we go, spinning down, seemingly out of control, our lives becoming defined by this endless cycle.

Depressing.

Unless. Unless there is a way to interrupt it.

How many of us are spending all our energy in conversations and counseling and prayer, trying to shift the most visceral thing about us— our emotions—yet having no success?

If you feel sad and I tell you to quit feeling sad, has any progress been made?

What if, instead of spending our energy trying to fix the symptoms, we went to the root of the problem, deeper even than the emotions that seem to kick off our cycles? The reality is that our emotions are a by-product of something else.

Our emotions are a by-product of the way we think.

EMOTION

THOUGHT

BEHAVIOR

RELATIONSHIPS

CONSEQUENCE

What's good about this news is that we can change our thinking. The Bible tells us so. "Do not be conformed to this world," one verse says, "but be transformed by the renewal of your mind."[5]

My deep dive into the inner workings of the brain confirmed what the Bible says: we can take every thought captive. Not only can our thoughts be changed, but *we* can be the ones to change them.

The problem is, we get on this spiraling train, often unaware of where our thoughts could eventually lead. The well-known Puritan theologian John Owen said that the enemy's goal in every sin is death. His actual words were "Be killing sin or it will be killing you."[6] It's time for us to fight.

The average person has more than thirty thousand thoughts per day. Of those, so many are negative that "according to researchers, the vast majority of the illnesses that plague us today are a direct result of a toxic thought life."[7]

The spiral is real and stuffed with more thoughts than it seems we can manage.

But what if, instead of trying to take every thought captive, we took just one thought captive?

What if I told you that one beautiful, powerful thought could shift this chaotic spiral of your life for the better . . . every time you thought it? What if you could grab hold of one truth that would quiet the flurry of untruths that has left you feeling powerless over your brain?

One thought to think. Could you do that?

Such a thought exists. More on that later.

I understand that despite the straightforward nature of my ask—that you take hold of one truth to focus your mind—fulfilling it is no small thing. Why? Because a full-fledged assault is taking place in those folds of tissue that make you who you are. **The greatest spiritual battle of our generation is being fought between our ears.**

What we believe and what we think about matters, and the enemy knows it. And he is determined to get in your head to distract you from doing good and to sink you so deep that you feel helpless, overwhelmed, shut down, and incapable of rising to make a difference for the kingdom of God.

Even if you're one of those who won't be shut down and you are loving God and people as you go, a million toxic thoughts haunt you each step of the way.

Whether you find yourself shut down or just haunted by nagging discontent, here is my declaration on behalf of both you and me:

No more.

And I say "on behalf of both you and me" for a reason. The great irony is that while I thought God was directing me to all this great, ground-breaking information—how my friends could heal their lives by healing their brains and by thinking more thoughtfully about their thoughts—so that I could help everyone else, what I couldn't possibly have known at the time was that I was about to need this healing myself.

2

What We Believe

*A*T LEAST I'M NOT AS DUMB AS HER."
Those words were spoken behind my back by Derek in my sopho-more biology class.

Derek was three times the size of every other awkward fifteen-year-old in my grade, a guy everyone feared. I was a shy, quiet student who barely opened my mouth. How could he possibly find me dumb? The thing was, I *wasn't* dumb. I made all As and a few Bs with little effort—even in the most academically challenging classes.

I look back at that sophomore girl sitting there at the long science lab table and wish I could hold her face and tell her how not-dumb she is, but I'm not sure she would listen. Within an hour of Derek saying she was dumb, those tiny folds of tissue between her ears had built an entire case against her value, her security, her intellect, and her potential that would play on repeat for a decade to come.

A recent college grad with a degree in broadcast journalism, I was in-terviewing for a job at a news station. Two men from the station took my friend and me to dinner. They didn't want to talk about the job; they wanted to get to know us. After realizing they were hitting on us, I sat there and thought, *I will never be taken seriously in business by men.* That thought made me believe I did not have anything to offer as a woman in business. I built a case against my education, training, and gifts that would affect me for years to come.

My husband and I found ourselves in one of our first real fights as a newly married couple. He ignored me, and I slammed some doors pretty hard. He moved on, but I couldn't stop thinking, *He doesn't really love me.* And my mind started to build a case against our marriage.

After losing my temper with my eight-year-old son, I lay in bed later that night and thought, *I am failing as a parent.* For years, off and on, that thought twisted its way deeper into my mind.

The thing is, I have always believed lies. And not just believed them but built entire chapters of my life around them.

I'm pretty sure the same is true for you.

LIES WE BELIEVE

My friend Christina, a licensed therapist, tells me that Psychiatry 101 teaches therapists that when you and I choose to believe a lie about ourselves, it's one of these three lies we believe:

I'm helpless.

I'm worthless.

I'm unlovable.

Reflexively I tried to prove her wrong. "Seriously, Christina? Only *three*?" I told her that I've been known to believe three hundred lies about myself—in a day.

"Nope," she said. "Each one of those three hundred lies fits into one of these three."

For the sake of argument, let's assume that Christina is right. The question I have for you is this: Which of the three do *you* most relate to? Is there one you're more vulnerable to?

These lies—*I'm helpless, I'm worthless, I'm unlovable*—shape our thinking, our emotions, and the way we respond to the world around us. They trap us in their cycle of distraction and distortion and pain, preventing us from recognizing the truth we should believe. Most detrimentally, they change how we view God. **Every lie we buy into about ourselves is rooted in what we believe about God.**

Let's say I tend to feel worthless and invisible. And let's say I read Ephesians and learn that God, because He deeply loves me, chooses me and adopts me.[1] Even if I don't overtly deny the validity of that premise, I still doubt it is true for me. I nod at the truth, but I never fully absorb it and let it shape my identity.

Then let's say I am married to a spouse who is typically distracted with work. I don't feel seen in our marriage, which confirms my deep-seated fear that I am indeed worthless and invisible. So even in the most inconsequential of arguments with my husband, I feel anxious and start to spin every time he's short with me.

I can't see all that he has on his shoulders, I can't empathize with his stresses, and my needs exceed his ability to ever meet them.

Before long we are full-on fighting constantly, and we don't even know why.

My husband now has become the enemy in my mind and can't ever seem to say what I need to hear or be whom I need him to be.

And the spiral of my thoughts has now invaded my relationships and robbed me of joy and peace.

No human is ever meant to be the person who fills our souls or holds in place our worth. Only God can do that. But until I throw off the lie that God's love isn't for me, my emotions, decisions, behaviors, and relationships will remain twisted up in the mistaken belief that I'm worthless.

When we begin to think about our thoughts, perhaps for the first time, we can stop the downward spiral. We can reset and redirect them. That's our hope. Not that we would wrestle each and every fear, but that we would allow God to take up so much space in our thinking that our fears will shrink in comparison. I love the quote from A. W. Tozer that says, if God is "exalted . . . a thousand minor problems will be solved at once."[2] Sign me up. I want that.

Want to know a secret? We can have that. But please know that the enemy of our souls has no intention of releasing his grip on our minds without a fight. And let me tell you, he doesn't play fair.

Here we are just getting to know each other, and I'm about to let you in on some of the worst mental hell I've experienced. I'm preparing you now because it's heavy, and I don't much like heavy. I like fun and happy things. But if I don't take you into the darkness with me, then you might not believe me when I say that it is well worth the effort to face the recesses of our thoughts, believing that God can bring about life and peace.

I know this is possible, this shifting of our thoughts and in turn our lives. I know, because it's happened for me.

But before I discovered the thought that shifts us from turmoil to peace, I experienced the all-out attack of the enemy.

UNDER ATTACK

It was my first visit back home to Little Rock in several months. As I sat in the passenger seat of my mom's white SUV, I took in the familiar landmarks: my old high school, the Chili's restaurant my friends and I had frequented after football and basketball games, and the pool I always swam in growing up. I was reminded of just how comforting coming home can be.

Soon we arrived at our destination: a Baptist church where I was scheduled to deliver two talks with a book-signing event sandwiched between.

During my first talk I swung for the fences with the women seated before me. I was bold and clear in my presentation of the gospel message. "There's a real enemy with demons at his beck and call," I told the few thousand women gathered. "He wants to take you out. He's determined to steal your faith." I ached for them to experience the freedom Christ offers and for them to refuse to sleepwalk through their lives.

After that came the book signing, with the expected hubbub. Afterward I somehow found myself standing totally alone, something I try to avoid at large events for the sake of personal safety. The participants had already headed back into the auditorium to take their seats, conference organizers were buzzing around, tending to details, and staff were all covering their various posts. There I stood in the foyer, just me and one other person, a kind-looking woman I didn't know.

I realized I needed to get moving and find my seat ahead of the next session, which was about to start. I took two steps toward the auditorium when suddenly that kind-looking woman was in my face. Her expression darkened, her warm smile disappeared, and her eyes narrowed as she focused intently on me.

"We are coming for you," she said in an urgent whisper. "You need to quit talking about us. We are coming for you."

Her comments were so out of context that I couldn't sort out what she meant. "Ma'am," I said, "I'm confused. What are you talking about?"

With chilling certainty she said, "You know exactly what I am talking about."

"I'm sorry?" I said, still seeking clarity.

She repeated, "Quit speaking of us."

"I don't know what you're talking about," I said.

Again she said, "You know exactly what I am talking about." But I didn't.

And then I did.

I took several steps backward, turned toward the auditorium, approached one of the security guards who'd been asked to cover the event, and said with as much composure as I could muster, "The woman who's in the foyer just made threats against me. Can you please keep an eye on her?"

Moments later I took the stage and began my last talk. Partway through, I heard shrieking in the hallway that ran alongside the large auditorium. The tiny hairs on my arms stood on end as I briefly paused. I knew exactly who was screaming, and I knew exactly what this was about.

Figuring the security personnel would take care of the distraction, I launched back into my talk. This was just a crazy woman making empty threats. I would go home and forget all about it.

Then the devil overplayed his hand. While the woman was screaming bloody murder in the foyer, the power went out. I'm talking *all* the lights, the *entire* sound system, the *giant* screens behind me—everything. We were silent, there in the dark.

Did I mention that this was a huge megachurch with backup systems for its backup systems? On a sunny day during a heavily staffed event, the power doesn't just go out.

The screaming continued as we all listened, stunned.

"This has never happened before," the pastor of that church would later tell me. "The screaming you heard was that woman you pointed out to the guard, and her daughter. What was that all about?"

Dang.

I mean, I proclaim Jesus and I believe everything He taught. He taught about the enemy and showed His power over demonic forces. The enemy wasn't mysterious to Jesus. To Him, spiritual warfare was matter of fact. Jesus cast out demons regularly—that's what the Bible says.

But while I believe that there is a real devil and that he has real demons working for him and that a battle for our hearts and souls and minds is playing out all around us all the time, I'll tell you this: I'd never before seen such an undeniable manifestation of Satan's work.

The experience could have been terrifying, but instead, it had a different outcome initially: it made me wild with faith. I vividly remember that night. I talked about Jesus with everyone who would listen, including the waiter at the restaurant my family and I went to afterward and my sister's friends who happened to be in town. I was overwhelmed with how real and true it all was—God. Heaven. The enemy. This war we're in.

I'd never before been as sure as I was that day: *all* of this was true.

Which is why the spiral of darkness that followed caught me so incredibly by surprise.

3

Spiraling Out

ON MY WAY BACK TO MY PARENTS' HOME FROM THAT speaking engagement in Little Rock, I called Zac. He and I had been in an argument before I'd left town to go speak—about what, I don't remember, but I do remember my first words to him after he accepted my call were "Hey, babe. Fight's over, okay?"

While I had him on the phone, I began peppering him with questions: "How are our finances? Are we at odds with anyone? How are the kids?"

I actually used the phrase *circle the wagons,* as in "We need to circle the wagons, Zac."

What? Was our herd of cattle in danger?

The truth was, I didn't know where the danger might be. And I didn't exactly want to find out.

"Why are you worried, Jennie?" he asked. My anxiety was showing. I'm sure he was wondering, *What went down at that sweet Baptist church?*

I told him the story. And my never overly dramatic husband took me very seriously. Over the phone that night, we walked through all the parts of our lives that were within our control and made sure there wasn't an obvious place for us to be attacked.

We relaxed a little.

But starting that night—immediately after I experienced such absolute certainty in my faith—every night without fail, I'd wake at 3 a.m. in a momentary panic. *Ugh. Three o'clock again!* It's not that I'm not accustomed to waking in the middle of the night—what woman who has raised children isn't? But this time the wakefulness was different.

My mind was racing and it terrified me. I would circle for hours in the middle of the night.

It started with small thoughts and fears—wondering whether I was behind on laundry, worrying about one of my kids—but it would quickly move to bigger fears. *Is God real?* I was spending my life for Him, and that doubt suggested a terrifying possibility: that I was wasting my life.

In the dark, alone, in the quiet, I would push it away, but it seemed to yo-yo back into my brain, a nagging question I couldn't shake.

Ironically, my middle name is Faith, yet mine seemed to be eroding. Bible study teacher Beth Moore, a self-described "former pit-dweller," has said that there are three kinds of pits: the kind we jump into, the kind we accidentally slip into, and the kind we're thrown into.[1] This pit was the latter. I had been thrown in. The question that haunted me during those sleepless nights was how on earth to get out.

I've known people who at some point in their lives begin to doubt their career choices. Or they doubt whether they married the right person. Or they doubt their purpose in life. But what I was doubting went right to the core of who I was: I doubted the existence of God. Lying awake in my silent, too-dark bedroom each night, I doubted whether God was real.

If He was, did He really see me? Did He really love me? Did He care?

What was I thinking?

Of *course* God cared.

Didn't He?

THE WEIGHT OF MY THOUGHTS

When had the faith I'd proclaimed with sincere fervor seeped right out of me?

Who'd taken it? Where had it gone?

Would I ever get it back?

Suddenly, I was filled with doubt. Truthfully, it wasn't sudden. It was slow, subtle, almost imperceptible, growing slightly each night as I lay there in the dark.

My usually cheerful and optimistic demeanor was replaced by a lingering uneasiness. None of the methods I'd been taught over the course of my life about getting out of a funk were working. I was still working out and being productive at work and attending church. But my optimism was captured by a real, full-on war for my mind. I was being pulled under as these thoughts of doubt continued their relentless assault.

Eventually what began in the night slipped into the daylight. More and more I wondered whether it was all true, but in the daytime plenty of distractions exist.

Grabbing distractions—our brains are excellent at that.

And when it came to the moments I needed faith, I would choose it. I'd lean hard on the decades of my story with God—until I started to notice my passion eroding. My spiraling thoughts were dragging me into exhaustion.

Doubt steals hope. And with no hope, everything that matters doesn't feel as important anymore.

Have you ever been confronted with something so hard or heavy that it made you question everything you have believed?

I have since recognized that the enemy was at work, but in the midst of the downward spiral, I couldn't see it. My thoughts seemed to have control over me instead of the other way around. Looking back, I wish I could talk to myself, shake myself out of the toxic spiral I was in. There was a way out. And if you are in a small spiral or an all-out tailspin right now, I promise there is hope.

SINKING FAST

I'm helpless.
   I'm worthless.
   I'm unlovable.

There in bed, 3 a.m. attack after 3 a.m. attack, I'd somehow fallen prey to believing all three. Everything I'd believed before meant nothing. God meant nothing. Life meant nothing. I was helpless, because I was nothing. I was worthless, because I was nothing. I was unlovable, because who loves nothing?

The danger of toxic thinking is it produces an alternate reality, one in which distorted reasoning actually seems to make sense.

I thought about all the hard I had walked through in recent years. I'd watched one of my best friends suffer a series of massive strokes while also suffering an agonizing divorce, watched my sister Katie's world and marriage fall apart, endured wild challenges surrounding the adoption of our son Cooper from Rwanda, faced an onslaught of criticism from leaders I respect as I mustered the strength to launch an organization and lead a team for the first time, watched my husband, Zac, go through a terrifying bout with depression . . . The list went on.

Had my confidence in God's goodness been misplaced all this time?

In the wee hours of the morning, I began to hypothesize about where my life was headed. Had I given my life to a meaningless mission? Had all my effort and passion been for nothing?

Everything that once seemed so true and vital seemed to be fading away.

Around this time my family went to see the latest Avengers movie,

Infinity War. The movie has been out long enough that I don't feel bad about this spoiler: in the end some of my favorite superheroes just . . . *vanish,* crumbling to ash and blowing away as if they'd never been there, as if they'd never existed at all.

As if their lives meant nothing.

I sat in that theater, tormented by the idea that this was my destiny too. Whatever fulfillment I'd experienced, whatever impact I'd known, all of it was bound for vaporization. Nothing would matter in the end.

I would be in the dark, in a grave. The end. No God. No rescue. I was nothing. My life meant nothing.

Nothing mattered now. If there is no God, then who cares about anything?

(I told you it was going to get dark.)

For eighteen months straight—more than five hundred days—this is what I thought . . .

Until I learned to think differently about my thoughts. Until I remembered I had a choice.

4

Breaking Free

YOU'RE GOING TO THINK I'VE LOST MY MIND," I WAS telling my dear friends Esther and Ann, my cheeks still damp with tears, my hands shaking in my lap as the three of us perched awkwardly on the bench seats of a bus in a remote region of Uganda. "I mean, really. It's possible I've *actually* lost my mind . . ."

My choice to shoot straight with them about what I'd been experiencing—the months on months of 3 a.m. wake-up calls, the doubt, the unbelief, the terrifying sense that I'd lost my spiritual footing—was precipitated by their having observed my melting down thirty minutes prior in the office of the Ugandan officials we'd been meeting with. They'd watched as I came undone, so weary from fighting some unknowable force, so sick of pretending everything was okay when absolutely *nothing* was okay, that the only option I had was to tell them the truth.

So I spilled it. All of it. The weird encounter with the woman in Arkansas. The threat she'd made: *"We are coming for you."* The endless sleepless nights. The fear that I'd lost my faith, even though I don't believe it's possible for a person to lose her faith. My mouth spoke the words faster than my brain could process what exactly I was saying, as though I had pushed play on a secret recording I'd been making of the horror that had been my life for the past eighteen months.

"I don't know what I believe anymore," I said. "It's been dark . . . worse than I know how to say. I've been questioning everything for so many months. I don't know if I still believe God. I think that maybe I don't."

Ann studied my face with her characteristic intensity, waiting until I took a breath to insert her thoughts. "No. *No,*" she said. "I *know* you. I *know* your faith. I have walked with you and watched you all this time."

I looked at her, wide eyed, desperate for her perspective to be true.

"Jennie, this is the enemy," she said. "None of this is from God. This awfulness you've been experiencing . . . *this isn't who you are.*"

As her words pierced my inner chaos and penetrated my mind, I let my eyes fall shut and nodded my head.

Truth Breaks Through

The catalyst of my emotional meltdown in that Ugandan office was the startling experience of hearing a stranger proclaim intimately familiar words.

During many of those five-hundred-plus angst-ridden nights back home, the only solace I could find was in obsessively reciting a passage of Scripture that I hoped and prayed would keep me tethered to my faith in God. Years earlier I'd memorized Psalm 139, and there in the black darkness of my bedroom, my mind whirring with doubt and fear, I'd whisper these words:

> Where shall I go from your Spirit?
>   Or where shall I flee from your presence?
> If I ascend to heaven, you are there!
>   If I make my bed in Sheol [the grave], you are there!
> If I take the wings of the morning
>   and dwell in the uttermost parts of the sea,
> even there your hand shall lead me,
>   and your right hand shall hold me.[1]

I was banking on these words being true, specifically the ones where David, the author of this psalm, said that, try though we might, there is in fact no way to escape the presence of God. I wanted that to be true. I *needed* that to be true. So I'd whispered those words into the dark with desperate passion, again and again and again.

There in Uganda, my friends and I were visiting various refugee camps to observe the work being done by Food for the Hungry, an organization we all wanted to support in this effort. It was deeply gratifying to see the progress being made, even as I was in no shape to take it in. Our little team had come in from the field to a cramped office, where we were to meet with the in-country officials who were facilitating this good work. They were all believers, all passionate about the strides being made, all gracious and chatty and kind. "You'll join us for our devotionals first before our meeting?" one of the men had asked, to which we enthusiastically said yes.

I situated myself on one side of the un-air-conditioned room, across from Ann and Esther, and exhaled a thousand distracting thoughts. After a brief prayer the man opened his Bible and began to read. "O LORD, you have searched me and known me!" he said, his thick accent rolling over the r's. "You know when I sit down and when I rise up; you discern my thoughts from afar . . ."[2]

As these words emerged from his lips, realization sank heavy in me. *He's reading from Psalm 139—are you kidding me? He's reading from Psalm 139.*

"You hem me in, behind and before, and lay your hand upon me . . ."[3]

I felt myself brace as he spoke. I knew what was coming next.

"Where shall I go from your Spirit?" he said. "Or where shall I flee from your presence? If I ascend to heaven, you are there! If I make my bed in Sheol, you are there . . ."

Tears sprang to my eyes. The room grew stiflingly hot.

"If I take the wings of the morning and dwell in the uttermost parts of the sea, even there your hand shall lead me, and your right hand shall hold me . . ."

I knew that to excuse myself just then would have been inappropriate, even though I really did want to bolt. I felt my throat hitch and my eyes burn as dammed-up tears broke free. Here, halfway around the world, in a microscopic village we'd traveled a full day by prop plane and rickety bus to get to, I heard these familiar words from the mouth of a man whose native language is not English.

We loved the same God.

How could this God not be real?

This man could have read one of the other tens of thousands of passages, but here we were reading the very words—the only words—that were holding up my fragile faith.

When Ann said those simple words—*"Jennie, this isn't who you are"*—she was right. In my soul I knew it. This *wasn't* who I was. I loved God. I was a believer. I trusted Jesus and prized my faith. And God was not going to let go of me.

The fears.

The doubts.

The restlessness.

The pain.

None of it was who I was.

God is real, and I am valuable.

My life matters.

He is real.

I had an enemy, and I'd let him beat me up for too long.

I was over it.

This was war.

CLEAR VISION RESTORED

After Ann and Esther and I returned home from Uganda, Ann laid out our plan of attack. Part of me felt like a bother to my good friends, but the rest of me was desperate for help.

Ann decided that for twenty-four hours the three of us, to stand in solidarity against whomever or whatever had pulled me so deep into the pit of unbelief and doubt, would together pray and fast from all food and drink.

No morning smoothie. No Torchy's Tacos for lunch. No late-afternoon Starbucks—the flat white or the madeleines. Water—that was it. For a full day we'd take the energy that usually went into thinking about food, preparing food, and eating food and direct it instead toward prayer. We'd pray for my confidence. We'd pray for my steadiness. We'd pray for my faith.

It all was way too self-focused for me, but given the fear and pain I'd been dealing with, I was all in.

In the days following Uganda, I must have replayed that comment of Ann's a thousand times.

"This isn't who you are."

How could one simple declaration, one simple reminder, unlock the thick chains binding my mind and my heart for over a year?

I thought about something the apostle Paul (known also by his Hebrew name, Saul) experienced upon coming to faith in Christ. He'd been a persecutor of Christians until he encountered Jesus on the road to Damascus, where he'd fallen blind. For three days, Acts 9 says, Saul ate nothing, drank nothing, and saw nothing. He had been directed by Jesus to go into the city and wait for further instruction. So the blind man, being led by his traveling companions, did as he was told.

Eventually a disciple from Damascus named Ananias came and laid hands on Saul. And he said, "Saul, the Lord Jesus who appeared to you on the road by which you came has sent me so that you may regain your sight and be filled with the Holy Spirit."

"Immediately something like scales fell from [Saul's] eyes, and he regained his sight."[4]

Saul rose.

Saul was baptized.

Saul ate a meal.

Saul gained strength.

It is no exaggeration to say that upon hearing Ann's words—*"This isn't who you are"*—I could see something I hadn't been able to see in months.

Because alone in the dark the devil can tell you whatever the hell he wants.

Now I wasn't alone. I was fighting, and in Christ I was given the authority and power to win.

Something like scales fell from my eyes, and finally I had vision again.

I'd had an encounter with truth, and while "the natural person does not accept the things of the Spirit of God, for they are folly to him, and he is not able to understand them because they are spiritually discerned," as Paul said, we have the mind of Christ.[5] The spiritual person is led by truth. Even when that spiritual person has been in the dark for what seemed a very, very long time.

I knew Ann had been right.

THE MOMENT OF CHANGE

Interestingly, during those months of torment, everything about my public life had screamed of a sincere, rooted faith. I had proclaimed Jesus with unabated passion and seen the miracles of lives changed, all the while fighting to hold on to my faith.

I was actually full of faith.

An Important Note

You may live with low-grade sadness and have for as long as you can remember. Or maybe for you, it's far worse than that.

Two people in my life who love Jesus deeply are fighting regular desires to take their own lives.

With the National Alliance on Mental Illness reporting that "one in 5 adults experiences a mental health condition every year,"[6] it's safe to say that mental illness is rampant. If mental illness is a struggle you face, may I please wrap loving arms around you, look you in the eyes, and whisper, "This—your anxiety or depression or bipolar disorder or suicidal thoughts—is not your fault"?

You may be suffering from a true chemical breakdown in your body. I get that. Several members of my family depend on medicine to help regulate their brain chemistry. Please hear me: there is no shame in that choice. Praise God for tools that help.

I just want you to know—please, lean in close and hear this—that throughout this book, whenever I talk about God giving us a choice about how we think, I am not suggesting that you can think your way out of mental illness. I am not. I have experienced seasons of anxiety so brutal that I was paralyzed.

There are seasons when we need help in the form of counseling and medicine. But I hope to show you in the coming pages that in every season there is help that we can access for ourselves. Learning to think a single thought can help us all—those of us who struggle with mental illness and those of us whose struggles are of a different sort.

I just didn't feel very full of faith.

What I felt was very beaten up.

The tragedy for me was I didn't have to be spinning out for eighteen months. Neither do you. We don't have to spin out for eighteen months. We don't have to spin out for eighteen *minutes*. We don't have to spin out at all.

I hesitate to say this next thing for several reasons. Maybe you're skeptical. Maybe you've fought specific bondage your entire life, and my answer will seem pat. Maybe you can't even *imagine* freedom, let alone work to pursue it. But I am going to say it anyway. I'm going to say it because it is true:

You can, in fact, change in an instant.

You.

And I.

Can change.

Science proves we can. Our brains are full of neural pathways, some shallow and moldable and some grooves dug deep from a lifetime of toxic thoughts. In both cases, God is mighty to save. In both cases He's mighty to heal.

After our period of fasting and prayer, my brain felt newly awake and my thinking sharp and clear, as if I'd been peering through a heavy fog that suddenly lifted. I set out to understand what Scripture tells us about our minds.

I started studying, and the first verse that I began to dissect was from Paul, a verse we touched on briefly earlier. "Do not be conformed to this world," he said in Romans 12:2, "*but be transformed* by the renewal of your mind, that by testing you may discern what is the will of God, what is good and acceptable and perfect."[7]

Do you want to be transformed? I don't know why else you would be reading this book. Is there another reason? I mean, Netflix is beckoning, dishes are in the sink, and there are ten thousand other things you could be doing. Yet you're here. So I'm guessing you are here because you actually hope to be radically different somehow.

We are going to attack something most sane people wouldn't dare to fight. Worse still, the reason they don't fight it is that they don't even recognize the fight is happening. They don't realize there is an all-out assault against them. They don't see the enemy coming for them. They don't know they're about to get trampled. They're living completely unaware.

That was me for a year and a half. But then came the moment when truth pierced my darkness—and everything shifted.

But let's not be naive: **if our thought lives are the deepest, darkest places of stronghold within us, all hell will try to stop us from being free.**

We aren't going to slap on strategies. No, we are going to go to war against the root of darkness within us. And we're going to have to dig deep to pull that root up.

This is going to take work.

This is going to take patience.

This is going to take buckets of grace for ourselves.

After I told my friends about my eighteen-month spiral of doubt, because of how urgent it was, we threw at this beast of a spiral everything, spiritually speaking, that God gave us in our arsenals. I saw healing quickly when I recognized the attack of the enemy and began fighting back.

In other spirals, where grooves have been dug deep, healing is taking place over time. But in all cases, the weapons we fight with are the same. Day by day we fight to be the captors of our thoughts rather than the ones taken captive.

While I was typing the previous section, I got a text from my friend who told me that my website had been hacked by a porn site. Yep. As I am talking about going to war with the devil, he goes to war with me.

Coincidence?

I don't think so.

5

Where Thoughts Are Captured

A S I MENTIONED EARLIER, CAPTURING ALL OUR THOUGHTS seems an impossible task, especially when we consider our potential number of thoughts per minute. Based on that thirty thousand thoughts a day and sixteen waking hours, we might think about thirty-one thoughts per minute. Remember what I said about taking just one thought captive? What if one thought held the power to interrupt our spirals and bring peace to our mental chaos?

Paul's own life was a picture of interruption. After the scales fell from his eyes, Paul's life and mind centered on an entirely new reality. There was no other hope, no other narrative, no other track playing in the background. He stopped the things that had distracted him and let himself focus on one simple thing:

"To me to live is Christ," Paul wrote in Philippians 1:21, "and to die is gain." It's all—always—about Christ.

Paul experienced a massive shift, and now he was a totally different man. No longer was he a slave to his circumstances or his emotions. Paul now chose to live aware of the power of Christ in him, through him, and for him. Paul now had the power of the Spirit—the same power that raised Jesus from the dead,[1] and he chose to live aware of and under that power.

In what may be the most provocative explanation in Paul's entire New Testament litany of provocative explanations, the apostle had this to say:

> Though we walk in the flesh, we are not waging war according to the flesh. For the weapons of our warfare are not of the flesh but have divine power to destroy strongholds. We destroy arguments and every lofty opinion raised against the knowledge of God, and take every thought captive to obey Christ, being ready to punish every disobedience, when your obedience is complete.[2]

In the late Eugene Peterson's paraphrase, that last bit reads like this:

> We use our powerful God-tools for smashing warped philosophies, tearing down barriers erected against the truth of God, fitting every loose thought and emotion and impulse into the structure of life shaped by Christ. Our tools are ready at hand for clearing the ground of every obstruction and building lives of obedience into maturity.[3]

Here's what I take from these words: You and I have been equipped with power from God to tear down the strongholds in our minds, to destroy the lies that dominate our thought patterns. We have the power and authority to do this!

Yet we walk around acting as if we have no power over what we allow into our minds.

If our toddler is throwing a fit in the grocery store, we correct him, redirect him—yet we have allowed our minds to have outright meltdowns with zero correction.

For eighteen months straight, I thought I was a victim of the arguments against God rising within me. For too many years of my life, I thought I was a victim of the negativity rising within me. Do you relate to what I'm saying? Have you also spent way too much of your life believing you are a victim to your thoughts?

Paul tells us that we don't have to live this way, that we can take captive our thoughts. And in so doing, we can wield our power for good and for God, slaying strongholds left and right.

THE INTERRUPTING THOUGHT

This promise of wielding power over our thoughts sounds great, doesn't it? Yet I sense a small question from you:

"Um . . . how?"

As in, "Thanks, Jennie. Sounds terrific. But how on earth do I get that done?"

Throughout the coming chapters you and I will learn how to go to war with the weapons that God has given us, weapons that can take out seven strategic enemies that attack us and undermine our efforts to maintain steady, sound minds.

The big picture here is this: We have chaotic thought lives. These thoughts often lead to wild emotions, true? Emotions that tell us how to behave.

Those behaviors dramatically affect our relationships, continuing that downward spiral we looked at previously.

What we're saying, then, is that *how we think* directly results in *how we live.*

This may sound terrifying, but, in fact, it's exciting.

You'll have to trust me for now.

This is what I know: while we may not be able to take every thought captive in every situation we face every day, we can learn to take *one* thought captive and, in doing so, affect every other thought to come.

So what is the one thought that can successfully interrupt every negative thought pattern? It's this:

I have a choice.

That's it.

The singular, interrupting thought is this one:

I have a choice.

If you have trusted in Jesus as your Savior, you have the power of God in you to choose! You are no longer a slave to passions, to lusts, to strongholds, to sin of any kind. You have a God-given, God-empowered, God-redeemed ability to choose what you think about. You have a choice regarding where you focus your energy. You have a choice regarding what you live for.

I have a choice.

We are not subject to our behaviors, genes, or circumstances.

We are not subject to our passions, lusts, or emotions.

We are not subject to our thoughts.

We have a choice because we are conquerors who possess weapons to destroy strongholds.

Now, we rarely get to choose our circumstances, but Paul said we have a choice about how we think about those sometimes-challenging things. And I love that truth. I love that truth because so often I sit down with women, and I hear their stories, and it doesn't matter what country or city we're in, the struggles are the same. I'm talking to women in huts in Uganda. I'm sitting on the mud floor with them, with interpreters, and they are talking about the same fears for their kids that I have for mine.

The people who stand out to me are the ones who have chosen to trust Jesus more than trusting their ability to make everything work out fine.

These heroes of the faith are not subject to their own thoughts.

They are not subject to their feelings.

They believe in one chief aim, and with every ounce of their power, they are working to think about Christ.

Jesus is the axis around which all their thought spirals spin. When their minds turn and turn, they fixate on Him.

Which prompts the question "What do you fixate on?"

You know your fixation. It is the thing you constantly think about. Come on.

My besties know my fixations because those fixations aren't easily hidden. Our fixations come out in our words, in our feelings, and in our decisions. They are the focus of the books we read, the podcasts we subscribe to, the websites we scour, the groups we join, and the obsessions we pursue.

Are you fixated on the fear that your kid will someday rebel? You're going to read a lot of parenting books.

Are you anxious about getting sick or not being uber-healthy? You'll listen to tons of health podcasts and spend a small fortune on essential oils.

I've written before about the eating disorder I wrestled with in college and for several years afterward. It started when I was a cheerleader at the University of Arkansas and we were weighed every week. If any of us on the squad gained more than three pounds in the week prior, we got benched for that week's game.

I was *obsessed* over meals. Over working out. Over what to eat and what not to eat.

Those weigh-ins stopped, but my obsessiveness didn't. My fixation became a place I felt tragically stuck in.

Then I read Paul's famous words: I could take my thoughts captive to the obedience of Christ.

My mind was blown.

My spiral was interrupted.

I had power over my life and mind again.

God has given you the power to interrupt this fixation! That's what that verse from Paul said to me. That was news I desperately needed to hear.

The question that remained was, How? *How* could I interrupt my downward spin?

For you, the answer, at least in part, might lie in counseling. Or in community. Or in fasting. Certainly, in prayer.

For you and me both, the answer will center on God—on His presence, on His power, on His grace, on His Word.

Every spiral can be interrupted. No fixation exists outside God's long-armed reach. Because we are a "new creation," we have a choice.[4]

He has given us the power and the tools and His Spirit to shift the spiral. When we're willing to take the initiative here? Some pretty cool stuff starts to unfold.

When we think new thoughts, we physically alter our brains.

When we think new thoughts, we make healthier neural connections.

When we think new thoughts, we blaze new trails.

When we think new thoughts, everything changes for us.

A MENTAL RESET

One author I came across in my studies about the brain was Dr. Dan Siegel, a professor of clinical psychiatry. "Where attention goes," he wrote, "neural firing flows and neural connection grows. . . . Patterns you thought were fixed are actually things that with mental effort can indeed be changed. . . . We are not passive in all this activity of mind and awareness."[5]

What we think about, our brains become. What we fixate on is neurologically who we will be.

It all comes down to a thought.

And then another thought.

And then another thought after that.

Tell me what you're thinking about, in other words, and I'll tell you who you are.

Take my son Cooper, for instance. He's ten. Whenever he starts spiraling, his mind, body, and emotions going down, down, down, I work to interrupt the spiral. I work to help redirect his thoughts.

"Buddy, time out," I tell him. "I love you. You're okay. You don't have to panic. You can choose another way. You don't have to be steamrolled by this."

I tell Cooper what is real.

I tell Cooper what is true.

And then I try to remember that what's true for him is also true for me.

Want in on a secret? That stuff is true for you too. You and I redirect children all the time. Why don't we redirect ourselves? First, of course, we have to remind ourselves that change is possible. Let me say it again: we have a choice! And the more often we grab hold of that truth, the easier it will be to interrupt the downward spiral of our thoughts.

As I've been practicing the patterns we're about to walk through together, shifting my thoughts has become more disciplined. Look at the spiral graphic on the next page. Starting from the bottom this time, with emotions and thoughts about to spiral out of control, see how we can stop and change them by choosing the mind of Christ.

Paul's words in Romans have never been more real to me than in this fight: "For I delight in the law of God, in my inner being, but I see in my members another law waging war against the law of my mind and making me captive to the law of sin that dwells in my members."[6]

This is a daily battle! I may not be doing it perfectly, but I have seen significant improvement. The change that once felt impossible, probable at best, was now in plain sight.

CONSEQUENCE

RELATIONSHIPS

BEHAVIOR

THOUGHT

I HAVE A CHOICE
THE MIND OF CHRIST

EMOTION

Where are you and I headed? We're aiming for one step beyond even that. Based on Paul's writings long ago to the church in Rome, you and I can learn to mind our minds to the point that controlling our thoughts becomes reflexive—an automatic, intuitive response.

In Romans 8:5 Paul said that "those who live according to the flesh set their minds on the things of the flesh" and that "those who live according to the Spirit set their minds on the things of the Spirit." He went on:

> To set the mind on the flesh is death, but to set the mind on the Spirit is life and peace. For the mind that is set on the flesh is hostile to God, for it does not submit to God's law; indeed, it cannot. Those who are in the flesh cannot please God.
>
> You, however, are not in the flesh but in the Spirit, if in fact the Spirit of God dwells in you. Anyone who does not have the Spirit of Christ does not belong to him. But if Christ is in you, although the body is dead because of sin, the Spirit is life because of righteousness. If the Spirit of him who raised Jesus from the dead dwells in you, he who raised Christ Jesus from the dead will also give life to your mortal bodies through his Spirit who dwells in you.[7]

I have read and reread this passage in the past few months, mulling over how life would be if I could truly have a mind that dwells on the Spirit. A mind that is full of life and peace. A mind that consistently thinks about God—who He is and what He wants for me. I so desperately want the "perfect peace" God promises when my mind is fixed on Him.[8]

Again, not perfectly but more regularly thinking this way.

I want to be so well versed in the patterns of thinking in line with the Spirit that my default is not to rely on the flesh but on the Spirit in everything.

This is the goal of our deliberate interruptions: we abruptly stop the crazy spirals of our minds.

As we practice the art of interruption, we're shifting to a whole new mind-set, and with each shift we will find ourselves growing more and more into the mind of Christ.

When we're spiraling in noise or distractedness, we have a choice to shift our minds back to God through stillness.

When we're spiraling in isolation, we have a choice to shift our minds back to God through community.

When we're spiraling in anxiety, we have a choice to shift our minds back to God through trust in His good and sovereign purposes.

When we're spiraling in cynicism, we have a choice to shift our minds back to God through worship.

When we're spiraling in self-importance, we have a choice to shift our minds back to God through humility.

When we're spiraling into victimhood, we have a choice to shift our minds back to God through gratitude.

When we're spiraling in complacency, we have a choice to shift our minds back to God through serving Him and others.

I should tell you here that after the day of prayer and fasting that led to my becoming obsessively vigilant about practicing the Paul-like patterns you'll read about in part 2 of this book, I've never again woken up terrified. For a full year now, those 3 a.m. wake-up calls are no longer paralyzing me.

In the same way, you may find that some thoughts, once interrupted, will simply lose their power. God can do this.

Other thoughts, however, may require daily capturing and redirecting. Or hourly. In some cases, more often than that. But those deadly thoughts can be captured. They can be contained.

We can be set free from the steepest of spirals.

We can learn to mind our minds.

We can live as if we have a choice in this matter, because we *do,* in fact, have a choice.

A heavenly Father gave everything for me to be free. Everything so I could choose this way out! He built the way out with the love and blood of His Son, Jesus. When we think thoughts that lead to life and peace, we don't just get better thoughts, we get more of God.

We may still wake in the wee hours of the morning when all around us is dark. But rather than squirming and stewing and letting evil scenarios run haywire through our minds, we can meet with God, be reminded of His kindness, and pray.

The battle for our minds is won as we focus on Jesus—every moment, every hour, every day.

6

Make the Shift

A FEW MONTHS AGO, I GATHERED A ROOM FULL OF WOMEN in my local church to study the things you and I are talking about here. We met for six weeks, and lives were changed. The first night those women streamed into the chapel where we were meeting, they were greeted by a giant whiteboard on which was written the question "What are you thinking about?" Attached to that board were dozens of brightly colored sticky notes with topics that might be taking up space in their thoughts, things like these:

- others' opinions
- finances
- plans
- the holidays
- the weekend
- the news

Before the women in the Bible study took their seats, they were asked to identify a few of the thoughts that were true for them and peel off those sticky notes. It was a challenging task.

Following that evening's exercise, my team and I assessed which thoughts had been taken and by how many women and which thoughts were still left on the board.

If you ask Mr. Google how many of our many thoughts per day are positive and how many are negative, you will discover that the vast majority—a full 70 percent, some researchers say—are negative.[1]

Back at the chapel, despite dozens of positive options available on those sticky notes, guess which options got picked?

- stress at work
- stress over finances
- Am I good enough?
- Am I worthy?
- failures
- rejection
- pain

Guess which stickies remained untouched?

- choosing joy
- strength
- good memories
- my heart

"Hiking" did get three takers, so at least there's that.

Now, I've got to tell you, based on what these women indicated they were thinking about, I pretty much knew what assumptions they were making. Assumptions such as *If people knew how badly I'd failed, they'd never love me* and *My worth comes from my ability to be perfect. No wonder I am not worthy of much.*

As a result of those assumptions, emotions surface: frustration, anger, despondency, hopelessness, embarrassment, inadequacy, shame.

From those emotions, beliefs begin to form: *I'll never thrive in my career. I'll never be good enough. I'll never be accepted and loved. I'll never get out of debt.*

From those beliefs, actions are taken: We will numb our pain. We will hide our fear. We will fake our happiness. We will "armor up."

Those actions over time form habits, which craft the lifestyles that shape our days.

No wonder so many of us have trouble sticking to change! We fall prey to that 70 percent negative thinking and then wake up one day utterly defeated.

We need a new normal, something those sticky notes only served to confirm.

It's true that for some people, including maybe you, their central emotion in a given moment is something like peace or contentment or joy. But give those same people a day or a week or a month, and trouble will have its way. It always does, you know? We live in a troubled world.

As Jesus said, "In this world you will have trouble."[2]

The good news is this: once we recognize that a prevailing emotion is connected to outright, life-sucking lies, we begin to see that everything we need for life in God has been given to us already[3]—which means we begin to heal and live lives that matter.

Over the past year, since my return home from that trip to Uganda with Esther and Ann, I've taken to calling this escape plan "the shift." When I'm mired in a certain way of thinking that clearly is not serving me well, I can escape that thought pattern and seize a new thought pattern. I can make a mental shift. And by changing my mind, I can change my emotions, which interrupts that entire progression we looked at earlier that results in *how I'm experiencing life.*

The best part? You can do the same. You don't have to spiral downward and end up in a panicked heap. You don't have to be held captive by fears and doubts. You don't have to dwell on every horrible thing that may never happen.

According to Paul, in order to make the shift from "warped philosophies" (a.k.a. overwhelming doubt) and "barriers erected against the truth of God" (a.k.a. 3 a.m. disbelief) to focus on something more in line with the "life shaped by Christ," we must take up the weapons of warfare and destroy the strongholds that are dominating our thoughts.[4]

First, of course, we must learn to recognize those strongholds.

Your Mental Story Map

We begin by being aware of what we are thinking about, by zeroing in on the thought and identifying it for what it is. Evil never wants to be noticed, I should mention here. It sneaks in and hijacks our minds, and we barely notice anything's amiss. I barely noticed, anyway.

So a vote for noticing. For thinking about what we're thinking about.

If you're game to give the thinking-about-thinking thing a try, then grab a journal and a pen. Ready?

Step 1

Referring as needed to the graphic example, write in the center of a blank page the primary feeling or emotion you're experiencing right now. It could be good or bad.

You might write *anxious.*

Or *peaceful.*

Overwhelmed.

Angry.

Afraid.

Whatever it is, jot it down. Now draw a big circle around that word.

Scattered around that large circle, write everything you can think of that is contributing to that feeling or emotion. You might write "Laundry that isn't done" or "Work" or "Kids" or "Financial stress" or "Body-image issues." Draw a smaller circle around each of these contributing factors; then trace a line from each of them, connecting them to the large one. Nearby each small circle, list how that factor has been contributing to the emotion you're experiencing.

- PROJECT DUE TOMORROW
- DISAGREEMENT WITH COWORKER
- FEEL INADEQUATE FOR MY JOB

WORK

FAITH — **OVERWHELMED** — **FRIENDS**

- FEEL DISTANT FROM GOD
- NOT DOING ENOUGH FOR GOD
- EXCITED ABOUT MY NEW SMALL GROUP

- LONELY LATELY
- FEEL LIKE I GIVE AND GIVE WITH NO RETURN
- EXCITED ABOUT A FEW NEW FRIENDS

HEALTH/BODY

- FEELING INSECURE ABOUT MY WEIGHT
- WORRIED ABOUT THE DOCTOR'S APPOINTMENT
- ANXIETY FLARING UP LATELY

Keep going until you have exhausted all the possibilities prompting the emotion you wrote down.

Step 2

Talk to God about it. Pray with your paper in front of you and talk through each thing you've written down. Go to His Word and look for the truths He's given us. Tell Him about it. Ask Him to show you what you are believing wrongly about Him and yourself.

Ready to move on?

Step 3

Look for patterns and common themes in your circles.

Are you worrying about things you cannot control?

Are you angry about how you've been wronged?

Are you obsessed with what you don't have?

Has food, sex, entertainment, or money taken over your thoughts?

Are you ashamed of what you've done in the past?

Are you self-critical?

Okay. So why did I have you go through this exercise?[5] It's so that you can see plainly how your thoughts are building a story line about God that is either true or untrue.

If we want to stop our patterns of toxic thinking, we must notice what's happening and take action, countering any lies we believe about God with the truth that interrupts the downward spiral.

And to do that effectively, we're going to need some help.

THE MIND OF CHRIST

It's almost impossible to navigate through our culture without being bombarded with messages about how we can do better and be better. "Experts" speak directly to our desire for hope through self-improvement books, websites, articles, infomercials, and so on. We feel a surge of optimism—the thrill of anticipation rises within us—when we hear how the right mantra, the right workout, the right financial plan, the right determination will lead us to the better, more fulfilling life we sense should be ours.

Who doesn't like to nip and tuck, to plan and resolve, to declare and push and grow? Who doesn't like the idea that with a little determination we can be better than we were before? None of us want to stay stuck where we are. We all want to flourish, to thrive.

Despite the wild success of today's lifestyle gurus, the idea of self-help is nothing new. Hundreds of years before Jesus's time, people were writing ethical arguments to help people choose wiser, better lives.

The self-help culture as we know it today has its most obvious origins in the nineteenth century. For example, in 1859 Samuel Smiles wrote a book that was titled, fittingly, *Self-Help*. You may recognize the famous maxim Smiles included: "Heaven helps those who help themselves." This message is so readily embraced that people have often been sure it's a quotation from Scripture. It isn't—the line is found nowhere in the Bible—but it might as well be. Who needs God when the real helper is inside us, is self? Ideas like this helped birth the self-help industry.

Time marched on, and others joined the cause.

Dale Carnegie released *How to Win Friends and Influence People.*

Psychotherapy grew more and more popular.

Infomercials became a thing.

Motivational speakers began to draw crowds.

And here we sit in a post-truth society bombarded with promises of happiness, wealth, fulfillment, and all our dreams met. Yet we are miserably unhappy. Why? Because **for all the good that self-help does, that help always comes up short in the end.**

The best that self-help can do with our suffering, with our shortcomings, with our spiraling is to reject it, to determine to do better, to declare, "Today this awfulness stops!"

But we don't simply need our spiraling thoughts to stop; we need our minds to be *redeemed.*

Bondage necessitates rescue.
Oppression needs to be lifted.
Blindness waits for sight.
Waywardness must be transformed.

No self-generated declaration—loud and passionate though it may be—can bring about this liberation. Instead, we need a complete transformation: our minds exchanged for the mind of Christ.

We are not made to think more good thoughts about ourselves. We are made to experience life and peace as we begin to think less about ourselves and more about our Creator and about others.

"Seek first the kingdom," Jesus said.[6]

The greatest commandments? Love God and love others.[7]

The only true self-help is for us as followers of Jesus to believe who we are as daughters and sons of the King of the universe and to know that our identities are secured by the shed blood of God's own Son.

When we believe that about ourselves, we think less about ourselves and more about the mission we have been given to love God and the people God puts in front of us, no matter our circumstances.

Sure, you can make a certain amount of progress on your own, but you're not going to have the fruit of the Spirit, and you're not going to have the mind of Christ. Are those who urge us to take control of our lives entirely wrong? No. We do have a part to play. But our effort won't take us across the finish line if there is no outside force shifting the inside of us.

What do you do once you take a thought captive? You then submit that thought to Christ. That is how you experience a new mind, a new identity, a new way to live, one that's Spirit empowered.

The world understands that no progress can be made without doing the work. They understand it better than many Christians do. **But self-help can offer only a better version of yourself; Christ is after *a whole new you.*** God in you. The mind of Christ. The fruit of the Spirit coming through you. You go from a dying, withered spruce tree to a thriving fruit tree producing pears. It's a completely new creation.

This work, this shift we're going to make, might be the most important thing we've ever done.

But we don't do it merely as another self-improvement project.

We do it because we want to live a new-creation kind of life, a life that truly matters, a life in Christ that God has promised.

Part Two

TAKING DOWN THE ENEMIES OF OUR MINDS

7

Drawing Battle Lines

AS WE HEAD INTO THIS PART, I WANT TO PULL YOU SUPER close and tell you what's about to happen and why.

I'm going to train you to fight.

Remember, the greatest spiritual battle of our generation is being fought between our ears. This is the epicenter of the battle.

Before Eve ate the fruit, she had a thought: it was "pleasing to the eye, and also desirable for gaining wisdom." And then "she took some and ate it."[1]

David, before he sinned with Bathsheba and had her husband killed, had a thought: "The woman was very beautiful."[2]

Before Mary birthed Jesus, she had a thought: "I am the servant of the Lord. Let it be to me according to your word."[3]

Before Jesus chose to go to the cross, He had a thought: "Father . . . not my will, but yours, be done."[4]

How we think shapes our lives.

Every great or horrible act we see in history and in our lives is preceded by a thought. And that one thought multiplies into many thoughts that develop into a mind-set, often without our even realizing it. Our goal is to be aware of our thoughts and deliberately build them into mind-sets that lead to the outcomes we want and the outcomes God wants for us.

One God-honoring thought has the potential to change the trajectory of both history and eternity. Just as one uninterrupted lie in my head has the potential to bring about unimaginable destruction in the world around me.

The battleground is not you yelling at your kids or cheating on your taxes or staring at your phone for hours on end.

The battleground is not even you serving at the local homeless shelter or joining the parking team at your church.

The epicenter of the battleground—the source of every word and deed that comes out of your mouth and life—begins in your thought life.

You aren't what you eat.

You aren't what you do.

You are what you think.

The Bible says, "As he thinks in his heart, so is he."[5]

Satan knows that we are what we think—so if we are believing things that are not true about us, then we are believing what the devil wants us to believe instead of what God wants us to believe.

You probably know what that one most recurring thought is for you, the one sticky thought that more than any other informs your other thoughts and, yes, your actions.

The enemy will tell you that change is hopeless, that you're a victim of your circumstances and your thought patterns.

The enemy wants you to settle, to find a way just to survive and be somewhat happy.

The enemy will urge you to accept that "this is just who you are," that your thinking is rooted too deeply in your personality or your upbringing to ever make a shift.

Your first objective is to capture the thought—to have the courage to face that defining, destructive thought and interrupt it: *I have a choice.*

Remember, this journey is not primarily about behavioral change, though that may be a by-product.

I can make no promises that this journey will change your circumstances. You may still lose your job, battle an autoimmune disease, or not find the perfect husband.

Taking every thought captive is not about what happens to us. It's about choosing to believe that God is with us, is for us, and loves us even when all hell comes against us.

But I have better news: capturing thoughts and then believing the truth will inform and shape every aspect of your life and give you peace and joy that transcend your circumstances. How? Because Jesus defeated sin, Satan, and death and rose from the grave, and because that same resurrection power indwells men and women who have been redeemed by the gospel.

This is a journey into joy that makes zero sense based on our circumstances.

This is a fight for clear, focused purpose amid rampant consumerism.

This is a God-given peace that surpasses understanding for our seasons of suffering.

This is redeeming the time amid unprecedented distraction and noise.

This is the beauty of esteeming others amid a narcissistic culture.

This is learning to speak the truth in love in a world that says we should never offend.

This is how you can breathe deeply and sleep peacefully in an anxiety-ridden society.

This is an otherworldly way to live.

You, as a believer, are a citizen of another reality. Let's learn to think like it.

In this part of the book, I want to offer a series of patterns that have helped position me for making the shift from negative, fleshly, worldly thinking to the supernatural but simple way the apostle Paul talked about—thinking that reflects the mind of Christ.

When we get confused about or distracted from the main point, we end up squabbling about inconsequential issues, using all our energy to fight the wrong enemy without realizing we've been duped. If we're not careful, we'll look up one day and realize we've been in the wrong battle all along. We'll find ourselves fighting against flesh and blood, when Scripture is clear in Ephesians that "we do not wrestle against flesh and blood, but against the rulers, against the authorities, against the cosmic powers over this present darkness, against the spiritual forces of evil in the heavenly places."[6]

If one of the greatest tools of the enemy is *confusion,* when we're confused, he wins the day. So let me spell out with crystal clarity where we're headed in the next part of this book—the problem we face, the mission we embrace, and the victory that's ours in the end.

THE PROBLEM

Every toxic thought, spiraling emotional cycle, and trap of the enemy we fall for somehow deep down involves a wrong belief about God.

I don't want to overcomplicate the problem. Romans 8 lays it out so clearly: a mind set on the flesh leads to sin and death, and a mind set on the Spirit leads to life and peace.[7] That is the simple reality we face.

But shifting our minds from flesh to Spirit is an ongoing work of the spiritual life. It is not a one-time decision but a day-by-day, moment-by-moment choice to move from chaos and confusion toward the peace of Christ in various areas of our thought lives.

Every enemy we are going to discuss here traces back to a core reality, which is that a battle is being waged for our lives. Standing between us and victory is one of three barriers—or perhaps all three:

- the devil
- our wounds
- our sin

Sometimes attack comes directly from Satan, and his strategy is obvious. He tempts with evil and loves to inflict suffering. Usually, however, he is sneaky. He tempts with successes and hypnotizes with comforts until we are numb to and apathetic about all that matters.[8]

Equally true, since we live in a fallen world, brokenness is our home (for now, anyway). We see this reality everywhere. In broken families and in longings that never seem to be satisfied, circumstances befall us constantly that scream, "Things are not as they should be!" Yet we hardly notice because this is the only home we've known. We tend to carry around deep hurt from our brokenness, rarely noticing it, never dealing with it or healing from it.

But as difficult as the first two realities are, the most common trouble we face in this life takes the form of sin. Specifically *our* sin—as in the stuff that you and I do. Or *don't* do, whichever the case may be.

Most of the time, you and I won't be taken down by a massive demonic attack. Our own small choices are accomplishing everything the devil intends—our passivity and destruction—with zero effort on his part. He is out "to steal and kill and destroy."[9]

Honestly it's often difficult to know which of the three is behind the attack, but bottom line: we are at war!

Hence the need for a targeted strategy.

THE MISSION

To defend ourselves in the midst of battle, we will learn to name the specific enemies we each are facing. I have identified seven enemies I see rampant and warring against our minds. We will learn to employ the right weapons at the right time to overcome the enemy, enjoy renewed intimacy with Jesus, and walk in greater freedom than we have before.

Whew. Big task.

Thankfully for us: *big God.*

We will name the lies that threaten us. We will learn to spot the signs that we've been sucked into the enemy's trap. We will learn to fight the war against our minds. We will learn what happens when we choose to shift our thoughts to God, to the truth of who He is and the truth of who we are because of Him. We will learn to seize things like community and service and gratitude as we live out the truth. And we will stand victorious in the end.

Which brings me to the secret weapon that ensures the outcome of our mission.

THE VICTORY THAT IS OURS

In Deuteronomy 20, God reminds Israel that He is with them in their battles and that He is with us:

Hear, O Israel, today you are drawing near for battle against your enemies: let not your heart faint. Do not fear or panic or be in dread of them, for the LORD your God is he who goes with you to fight for you against your enemies, to give you the victory.[10]

Ready for the good news? Through Jesus's sacrifice on the cross, God has rendered the fights we face His fights too. Because of Jesus, every fight has been ultimately won. Victory? It's already yours. It's already mine.

What's left for us is to claim that victory. We are going to look at both the enemies of our minds and the truths that set us free. If God is in us and is for us, then you and I can choose to fight from a place of victory. We can stand confident that God will prevail.

We have talked about what it means to take every thought captive, and we have talked about the one interrupting thought: *I have a choice.* Now we are about to go to battle against the unfettered thoughts that define us. Once the thought has been interrupted, we enter neutral ground.

We then get to decide whether we are going to choose life and peace, the mind of Christ, the fruit of the Spirit—or sin and death, the mind of the flesh.

In each of the next seven chapters, we are going to retrain our minds to think about truth. As we go to war with each toxic, twisted thought, we will begin to see the fruit and freedom of believing truth, walking moment by moment in our identity as children of God. The spiraling, chaotic thoughts that have so long kept us trapped will give way to the peace and beauty and abundant life Jesus died to give us.

Yeah, right. Quiet time with God.
Have you seen my schedule?

I'm not much of a space-and-solitude
kind of person.

I go crazy if it's too quiet.

I'm sure God has better things to do than
help me with my little problems.

I don't have time to slow down.

I'll feel better when I get
through my to-do list.

8

Holding Space for Silence

I Choose to Be Still with God

A FRIEND REACHED OUT TO ME NOT LONG AGO. SHE WAS spinning so fast emotionally that you could see it affecting her physically. I placed my hands on the outsides of her arms, as if to hold her up—or hold her still—as she spoke. Her marriage was in knots. One of her kids was acting out. Her pace of life was making her crazy. A misunderstanding had caused a rift between her and a dear friend.

I listened to her describe these struggles, and I knew I did not hold the power to stop her spinning in that moment. While there were a dozen or more practical problems to untangle, before any of that she needed the only thing that could bring peace. "I love you," I said as I looked into her eyes, "but you need Jesus right now."

Yes, there would be time for us to connect.

Yes, I would help in any way I could.

Yes, my friend would need the support of her people as she navigated the path ahead.

But now, first, while the rotations were coming fast and furious, she needed to be alone with God. She needed what only Jesus gives.

I said, "Right now I am going to leave you, and you spend thirty minutes alone with God."

She said she would.

In the stillness and quiet, not only do we connect with God but we are also able to more clearly identify what is wrong. Recognizing our spirals and naming them is the first step in interrupting them.

She had been spinning and desperate and dying for answers, yet when I checked in twenty-four hours later, the only thing she had to report to me were the twenty reasons that time alone with God just hadn't happened. Oh, and I get it. I am the same way!

Why is the simplest, best thing for our souls' long-term health so crazy difficult to do?

I'll tell you: because real, connected, intimate time with Jesus is the very thing that grows our faith, shifts our minds, brings about revival in our souls, and compels us to share Jesus with others. It's where the spiral stops.

To put it plainly: all hell is against us meeting with Jesus.

ESCAPE INTO BUSYNESS

During my own eighteen-month season of doubt and heaviness, I rarely chose time alone with God, outside of studying and preparing for Bible teaching. My tendency was to make it through the night and overcome the ensuing exhaustion with coffee and then more coffee after that, as I went careening through my day. If I could stay busy, my not-so-concrete thinking went, the doubt couldn't catch me. If I stayed distracted, I'd feel no pain.

Because if I slowed down enough to look at my soul, I might be overwhelmed by all that needed fixing in me. I didn't want to hear what God might want to say to me—or take the risk that He would remain silent, hidden, deepening my doubt about His existence, His love.

There are so many ways we avoid silence, so many types of noise we choose to fill the gaping voids in our souls. Social media is just the obvious one. We keep music playing in the car or streaming through our headphones. We pack our schedules with all the good things we think we should be doing. We juggle committees and demanding jobs and try to keep up with an unrealistic number of friends—yet we feel isolated. We are often doing so much for God but barely meeting with Him. And we feel as if we are failing everywhere we look.

Amid all this busyness, we've made it impossible to hear His voice saying, "Be still, and know that I am God."[1]

What is it that we're running from? What keeps us from carving out space and time for the quiet we so desperately need?

Ready for it?

Yes, we are busy and distracted and it is dang hard to sit still.

But we are also afraid of facing ourselves and, in turn, facing God.

We are afraid of being found out.

We forget that He not only loves us but actually likes us too.

Yep, He sees all; He even knows every thought before we think it, the psalmist said.[2] But somehow, unlike humans, He has grace for all.

Yet, just like Adam and Eve in the Garden of Eden, we find ourselves naked and afraid in life, so we choose to hide.

What are we afraid might be found out? Here are a few things I've seen, both in my own life and in the lives of those I know and love:

1. *The fear of being put to work.* Sitting alone with God has a way of bringing action items that we try so hard to avoid to the surface of our consciousness. Need to forgive someone who wronged you? Reach out to the person you hurt? Make good on a commitment you've been neglecting? Sitting in the quiet with God will remind you of these things and a thousand more.

2. *The fear of being asked to change.* Worse still, what if solitude reveals not just a specific action you need to take but rather a broader issue you need to repent of? The nightly numbing habit. The increasing tendency to yell at your kids. The pull of Facebook when you're being paid to work. If we don't carve out time when the Holy Spirit can help us assess the quality of our lives, then we convince ourselves we won't have to assess the quality of our lives. Easy, right? Yeah. Not the best approach.[3]

3. *The fear that you're all alone in the world.* Clearly this one hits closest to home. Why did I refuse to practice solitude during that eighteen-month span? Because I was afraid that if I reached out to God, there would be nobody home to take my call. I hate that I didn't close that distance sooner.

Quiet time isn't so quiet, is it? Our heads actually get noisier when the noise all around us falls away.

Behind every one of these fears is a lie: *I cannot face God as I am.* All we can see at first is the mess. Here's the truth: we are messed up, every one of us. Which is exactly why we need time with God alone, in the quiet, where we can hear His healing voice. We have a choice between chaos and quiet, between noise and solitude with God, between denial and healing.

So why is it dangerous to keep believing this lie? Because humans never stay in neutral. We are either moving toward something or moving away from something.

The antidote to running from ourselves is running to the only One who helps us get over ourselves. The lie is that we will be shamed. **The truth is that the God who is creator and sovereign over the universe and the God who conquered sin and death is the same God who wants to be with you in your pain, doubt, shame, and other circumstances.** "God's kindness is meant to lead you to repentance."[4]

LIE: I'll feel better if I stay distracted.

TRUTH: Only being with God will satisfy me.

> Better is one day in your courts than a thousand
> elsewhere.[5]

I CHOOSE TO BE STILL WITH GOD.

The thing that became abundantly clear to me, once I initiated contact with God again, was that the fears I'd harbored about connecting with Him were completely unfounded. This should have come as no surprise. If I were to ask you to complete the sentence "When we draw near to God . . . ," what truth follows it? *"He will draw near to us."*

The line is taken from James 4, from a passage cautioning believers against being overtaken by the ways of the world. The apostle wrote,

> Do you not know that friendship with the world is enmity with God?
> Therefore whoever wishes to be a friend of the world makes himself
> an enemy of God. Or do you suppose it is to no purpose that the
> Scripture says, "He yearns jealously over the spirit that he has made
> to dwell in us"? But he gives more grace. Therefore it says, "God
> opposes the proud but gives grace to the humble." Submit yourselves
> therefore to God. Resist the devil, and he will flee from you.[6]

And then in summary he wrote, "Draw near to God, and he will draw near to you."[7]

When we humble ourselves before God, submitting fully to Him, regardless of what has kept us away—and regardless of what we were doing while we were away and for how long we allowed that chasm to grow—we find He was always there, waiting for us to come back.

We Have a Choice

EMOTION
DISCONTENT

THOUGHT
I'LL FEEL BETTER
IF I STAY
DISTRACTED

BEHAVIOR
CONSTANT INPUTS

RELATIONSHIPS
NEEDY AND
FRANTIC

CONSEQUENCE
INSECURE

CONSEQUENCE
SECURE

RELATIONSHIPS
CALMING AND
REASSURING

BEHAVIOR
PRAYER AND
MEDITATION

THOUGHT
ONLY BEING WITH
GOD CAN SATISFY ME

I CHOOSE TO BE STILL

EMOTION
DISCONTENT

THE POWER OF FOCUSED ATTENTION

Friend, we were physically built for silence. God designed us this way, and science confirms that design. Secondary to the spiritual impact of time alone with God, according to the emerging field of neurotheology, quiet meditation quite literally changes our brains.

When we turn off the constant distractions and sit quietly before God, focusing intently on His Word and really meditating on it, a few things happen:

- Your brain will be physiologically altered. "Scientists have found that the brains of people who spend untold hours in prayer and meditation are different."[8]
- Your imagination will be rewired. "Inappropriate thoughts can be combatted with positive thoughts, such as thinking of a new hobby, playing music, repeating an inspiring quote, or some other positive activity," wrote Sam Black from Covenant Eyes.[9]
- The kind of brain waves present during relaxation increases, and anxiety and depression decrease. "Several studies have demonstrated that subjects who meditated for a short time showed increased alpha waves (the relaxed brain waves) and decreased anxiety and depression."[10]
- Your brain stays younger longer. "A study from UCLA found that long-term meditators had better-preserved brains than non-meditators as they aged."[11]
- You'll have fewer wandering thoughts. "One of the most interesting studies in the last few years, carried out at Yale University, found that mindfulness meditation decreases activity in the default mode network (DMN), the brain network responsible for mind-wandering and self-referential thoughts—a.k.a., 'monkey mind.'"[12]

- Your perspective will eventually shift. "When we take time to listen to what God has to say to us," wrote Bible teacher Charles Stanley, "we will see how much He loves us and wants to help us through every situation in life. He gives us the confidence to live extraordinary lives in the power of His Spirit and grace."[13]

Look back at the story of Saul encountering Jesus on the road to Damascus, and you'll see that as all other distractions—not just food and water but also *sight*—were removed from his life, he could *see clearly for the first time in his life*. Like Saul, when we turn our thoughts from our problems to the only One who holds the solution in His hands, we gain wisdom we'd not otherwise have. We gain insight we'd not otherwise experience. We find One who is *willing* to help us and *able* to help us and thus uniquely poised to intervene.

We come to see things not as they seem to us but as they truly are.

How many times have we created entire story lines based on worst-case scenarios? How often have we imagined someone's anger toward us simply because of a sideways glance that had nothing to do with us?

We build entire narratives that begin to take on lives of their own, based on assumptions and our overactive imaginations—all because we attend to fears, attend to distractions, attend to worst-case scenarios.

It has been said—and I think it is true—that the most valuable asset we possess is our attention, which prompts the question, To what are we attending?

Are we attending to our fear? Or are we attending to the God who promises to be with us?

Are we attending to our doubt? Or are we attending to the truth that never changes?

Are we attending to our need for control? Or are we attending to God's plan for us even if chaos breaks into the present reality?

I CHOOSE TO BE STILL ⟶

Are we attending to how we compare with others? Or are we attending to the gratitude we have for all God has done for us?

Are we attending to our worries regarding our health, our bank accounts, our careers, our spouses, our children, our regrets, our pasts? Or are we attending to the living God?

In my experience, we can do one or the other, but we can't do both at the same time. We will attend to the things that are crushing us, or we will take up the light burden that is Christ's. "Come to me, all who labor and are heavy laden," Jesus said, "and I will give you rest. Take my yoke upon you, and learn from me, for I am gentle and lowly in heart, and you will find rest for your souls. For my yoke is easy, and my burden is light."[14] *Come to me,* He says. *Be still and know that I am God.*

But First, Instagram

It's a typical Monday morning. I've gotten the kids off to school, and I'm craving time alone with God, longing for His input and His wisdom and His strength. If I were wired differently, I'd head back home after school drop-offs, and I'd pour a mug of hot coffee, tuck myself into the oversized chair in the living room, settle into the silent surroundings, and commune with Him . . . But I'm me.

I point my car toward our church and get there as fast as I (legally) can.

Our church is a massive place. The parking lot is big. The auditorium is big. The chapel is big. The coffee-bar area? Also big, which means that it can hold a big number of people at all times. I love big numbers of people, even on mornings when solitude is my aim. I park, head in, scope out a table on the covered patio, order a cup of coffee, and start to ease into a sloped-back wooden chair. Before my backside hits the seat, I hear a friend call "Jennie!" as she heads my way. *Ah, my people. Hello, hello!*

As I'm chatting with my girlfriend, another friend arrives and comes over to chat awhile. When the first friend excuses herself to take a call, an acquaintance of the second friend introduces herself. Things continue in this way, an unending flow of interactions and chats, a friend of mine happening by and then a friend of hers stopping to talk to us both, and before I know it, half an hour has passed. It's okay. It always goes this way. Given my unyielding extroversion, I need it to go this way.

As those acquaintances and friends head into the plans and conversations they've scheduled for the day, I reclaim the wooden chair. I tug my headphones from my backpack, the big cushy ones that leave no question in the minds of passersby regarding whether I'm "otherwise occupied." I slip them over my ears, pull out my Bible and journal and a pen, and for the next thirty or forty minutes encounter the living God. Well, just after I cycle through my feeds and inboxes: Instagram, email, Facebook, back to Instagram.

Sigh. Honestly, of all the hard work I've done this past year to take my thoughts captive, this has been the hardest of all—sitting down, all alone, in the hush. At the same time, the one pattern that has been most useful to me in the year since that Uganda trip is this same habit, the practice of time alone with God. Which is why I want to tackle it here at the beginning of our battle against worldly thought patterns.

This is where our thought lives change. **Connection with God is the foundation for every other God-given tool we have to fight with.** We begin here because if supernatural change is what we want, we have to go to our supernatural God to find it.

I want to look closer at Galatians 5, where Paul described the effects both of retreating from God's presence and of drawing near. "I say, walk by the Spirit, and you will not gratify the desires of the flesh," he wrote.

For the desires of the flesh are against the Spirit, and the desires of the Spirit are against the flesh, for these are opposed to each other, to keep you from doing the things you want to do. But if you are led by the Spirit, you are not under the law. Now the works of the flesh are evident: sexual immorality, impurity, sensuality, idolatry, sorcery, enmity, strife, jealousy, fits of anger, rivalries, dissensions, divisions, envy, drunkenness, orgies, and things like these. I warn you, as I warned you before, that those who do such things will not inherit the kingdom of God. But the fruit of the Spirit is love, joy, peace, patience, kindness, goodness, faithfulness, gentleness, self-control; against such things there is no law. And those who belong to Christ Jesus have crucified the flesh with its passions and desires. If we live by the Spirit, let us also keep in step with the Spirit. Let us not become conceited, provoking one another, envying one another.[15]

Now, it's easy to look at that litany of the works of the flesh and give ourselves a broad-brush pass. Because I don't tend to be tempted by sorcery or drunken orgies, I let myself off the hook regarding my own works of the flesh: my beloved Netflix, the fits of anger my kids seem to provoke in me, and the division between God and me I allowed for a year and a half.

How much I needed His presence.

I need it still now.

Why? Because even my best day pales in comparison with the reality He says I can live. And the same goes for you.

Because the fruit of the Spirit is our new way of being, Paul says we can be people who love—not just once in a while, but intentionally.

He says we can be joyous people. We can be people of kindness and patience and peace.

He says we can be good. Not to get some cosmic check mark but simply because our Father is good.

He says we can be faithful. *We don't have to waver in our faith.* Man, do I wish I could have stayed connected to this truth a year and a half ago. By God's grace I'll stay connected to it now.

He says we can be gentle and self-controlled.

But if you and I are to live this not just as a possibility but as an everyday, every-moment reality, we need to walk by the Spirit, not be jerked around by our swirling chaotic thoughts. In other words, we urgently need time in the presence of God.

"Father," we can say to Him, "help me see things not as they *seem* to me but as they truly *are.*"

WHAT ARE YOU REALLY THINKING?

When a group of us were talking about choosing time with God over our distractions, my friend Caroline, who is a senior at a nearby college, said to me, "Jennie, I know I am supposed to be thinking about God instead of all this chaos and clutter. One question: What do you think about whenever you think about God?"

I sat back, stunned by how the youngest woman in the room had just cut to the real question. You can't simply slap a cute cliché on this huge issue of thinking about God. If this is ultimately a call to dwell with Christ, then how do we practically get that done?

Remember that mind map I had you do earlier, where you noted the main emotion you were feeling and why? Let me show you how this practice of stillness, of solitude in the presence of God, is the basis of our strategy for interrupting all kinds of problematic thought patterns. As you look at your mind map, consider how simply thinking about God can shift these spiraling thoughts.

Let's say that you're buried under a pile of stress and angst because of some situations at work. Here is how the thoughts probably churn their way through your mind:

- I'm overwhelmed because I have way too much to do.
- I'm upset because I was passed over for the promotion I deserved.
- I'm anxious because I'm running behind on my project and letting people down.
- I'm frustrated because my boss is a micromanager.
- I'm angry because she was rude.
- I'm stressed because I'm working tons of hours yet not making ends meet.

Now, you'll notice a pattern in each of these thoughts:

[Negative emotion] *because* [reason].

- I'm stressed *because* I'm working too many hours.
- I'm frustrated *because* my boss doesn't trust me.
- I'm angry *because* she was rude.

What I want you to see in this and the next several chapters is that, with each weapon God has given us to wield in this battle for our minds, we get to rewrite that pattern while taking back the power He has given us.

In other words, we can cognitively reframe our situations with the new pattern looking like this:

[Negative emotion], *and* [reason], *so I will* [choice].[16]

- I'm upset, *and* I was passed over, *so I will choose* to remember that God has not forgotten me.
- I'm angry, *and* she was rude, *so I will choose* to meditate on God's kindness toward me.

- I'm overwhelmed, *and* I have too much to do, *so I will pause and choose* to thank God for existing outside the boundaries of time and for empowering me to accomplish only that which I need to do.
- I'm stressed, *and* I'm fearful about my finances, *so I will choose* to pray instead of fear.

When you're stuck in a downward spiral of distraction, what truth will you shift your thoughts to in order to combat the lie that anything can satisfy you like quieting yourself before God?

During a Bible study on the book of Philippians at our church, my friend Rachel surprised all of us with a spoken-word performance of a piece she'd written about guarding our hearts and minding our thoughts.

Within seconds of Rachel speaking, I realized maybe I could use fewer words in life, because she summarized five weeks of my teaching so poetically. Everyone related to her words, which means we aren't alone in our spirals. Is it possible we all have been fighting the same war? Here's what she shared with us:

The mind is a broken thing.
It runs, races, and paces, taking me places that
consume me, distract me, and tempt me to believe
I'm not good enough, no . . . never will be.

You've got to strive to survive,
to thrive, to stay alive in this world
of ever-changing, evolving ideals,
images, idols, and icons.

You have to work for your worth,
clean yourself up,

do more, be better,
don't show weakness, be tough,
try to be enough,
collect piles of treasures, trinkets, and stuff.
Maybe then . . . you'll be loved.

Yes, the mind is a broken thing.
If unguarded and let loose,
it can attack you and snatch you and trap you,
leaving you stuck, self-obsessed, asleep, and enslaved.

But "if anyone is in Christ, he is a new creation.
The old has passed away; behold, the new has come."
Your mind doesn't have to be out of control.
Those thoughts and loops and cycles can stop.

You're not left unarmed; you have a tool to interrupt
the racing, pacing, list making,
restless, unending, repeating, defeating,
distracting, disorienting, consuming, controlling thoughts.

Yes! You can interrupt and fight against the lies,
the arrows from the enemy that fly in the darkness of the night.
They are coming for you, but they don't want to be realized.
You have the Word, you have light, you have life.

Wake up from your twisted perspective that keeps you despairingly
    focused on yourself.
Instead, fix your eyes to see and know and understand what really
    matters.

You're not a victim of your own mind,
because if you're in Christ, you have victory.

A God who loves you, knows you, sees you, has shown you
a love so radical, intimate, personal, and wild
that He would painfully choose to lose a child
to reconcile all mankind. "While we were still sinners, Christ died."

It's hard to fully grasp the vastness of His steadfastness,
His mercy, and His grace that move past any mistakes that
        you or I have made
to pull us from the pit that we were once in.
And if you truly knew Him, you would love Him.
You would believe Him.
And you would kill any seed of a thought that would twist
        and thwart and take your mind from
whatever is true,
honorable,
just,
pure,
lovely,
commendable.

Yes, the mind is a broken thing,
But God's Spirit dwells deeper, His Word rings truer,
For in Christ Jesus we are free.[17]

We are free. Will we live in tandem with Him, aware of this reality?
Or stay in our brokenness?
    We have a choice.

People just aren't drawn to me.

If people knew how badly I had screwed up, they would run.

I'm not really a people person.

I've always been kind of a loner, and I like it that way.

People don't care about what I'm going through.

Nobody really gets me.

People don't need to hear about my problems.

9

Lifelines

I Choose to Be Known

JUST BEFORE ZAC AND I ADOPTED COOPER, OUR SON who spent the first four years of his life at an orphanage in the hills of Rwanda, we went through "adoption training." It wasn't called that, exactly, but that's what it was. We had never adopted a child, so we eagerly drank in every lecture, compelled to get this right.

All these years later, most of what I gleaned during those classes has faded from my memory, but one lesson wound itself around my heart so tightly that I imagine I'll remember it forever. The lesson was this: "If you want your child to thrive, then make him or her feel *seen and loved.*"

Feeling seen and loved—this is absolutely everything, the foundation and framework from which we build and thrive. When it's missing, everything around us seems to crumble into pointlessness and despair. As counselor and author Larry Crabb wrote, "No lie is more often believed than the lie that we can know God without someone else knowing us."[1]

We were built to be seen and loved.

When I was planning this book, dreaming about the impact it would have, I remember telling a friend of mine who is super into all things neurology about my vision for "all of America to shift their minds," for masses on masses of people to realize it really is possible to take their thoughts captive, for the *whole wide world* to finally start tearing down strongholds, and more. I was so passionate in my vision casting that I fumbled my words. My friend listened patiently, and when I eventually took a breath, she said, "You know, Jennie, nobody changes *anything* all alone with a book."

Ah. Gut punch. *Ouch.*

Of course, my friend was right. We can't curl up on our couches, read the pages of a book, pray, and simply *will* our minds to change. God is concerned not only with the posture of our hearts but also with the people on each of our arms. In terms of fulfilling our mission in this life, we can't do anything worthwhile alone.

God Himself exists in community, the Trinity relating as Father, Son, and Holy Spirit. Three persons, one God. Perfect community. Since God Himself lives in community, He formed us to need community too. The apostle Paul also gave many instructions regarding how we are to behave toward one another: "Love one another with brotherly affection. Outdo one another in showing honor." "Live in harmony with one another." "Comfort one another, agree with one another, live in peace." "Do not use your freedom as an opportunity for the flesh, but through love serve one another." "Be kind to one another, tenderhearted, forgiving one another."[2]

I've noticed that the idea of living in community is yet one more *instruction* we tend to regard as a *suggestion*. We may take a stab at it, but when things get tough, we push it aside.

Community is an essential. We find ourselves in a generation that has made an idol out of the very thing God is calling us away from: independence. The entirety of Scripture assumes community as a given in the life of a God follower. In the Old Testament, community develops within a people group, while in the New Testament it develops within local churches.

We are village people, built to be known and loved and seen. Nearly every people group in every generation has gathered around fires in communities that accomplish this, even if imperfectly.

Even today much of the world lives in villages. Recently my husband and I were in a small village in Europe and visited a grocer. The man at the counter wanted to know who we were and where we were from because he knows everyone who comes into his store. We were outsiders.

I wonder whether we—as the church, as Americans, as women—still view ourselves as village people, those who are known, noticed, loved, and seen. I think I know the answer. I think the answer is no.

THE TEMPTATION TO GO IT ALONE

The first enemy, distraction, keeps us from seeking help from God for the chaos in our heads. This second enemy, shame, keeps us from pulling others in to help.

I didn't mean to isolate myself in the spiral of doubt for eighteen months; I just never got around to expressing—aloud—what I was going through.

My friend Curt Thompson, a psychiatrist and brilliant thinker on everything related to the brain, says that no matter how strong someone looks on the outside, every person walking the planet has this deeply embedded fear that haunts them day by day. *If anyone really knew you,* the fear whispers, *they'd leave you.* This is the lie of shame. This is the lie that shatters your self-worth—the lie that reminds you over and over of the real you that you don't want others to see.

I don't know the exact words this fear uses to get to you, but if you're anything like the countless women I have spoken with over the years, then the terrorizing taunts probably sound something like this:

- *If people knew what I've done, they'd want nothing to do with me.*
- *If people saw who I really am, they'd run the other way.*

- *If people knew the thoughts I'm capable of thinking, they'd evict me from their lives.*

Or maybe the voice of this fear is more subtle:
- *Why would I bother people with my problems?*
- *I can handle this.*
- *What good will it do if I let someone in, anyway?*

When we listen to lies about our worth, we naturally back away from others. In many cases, our distancing behavior succeeds in pushing people away, reinforcing our fear of rejection. This is a classic mind trap, a self-fulfilling thought pattern in which our insecurity feeds our isolation, which in turn feeds the lie that we are worthless and nobody really gets us or cares to. We feel unseen and unloved, and to protect ourselves from further rejection, we won't let anyone close enough to change our perception.

Gradually we embrace the lie that we have to do life on our own, that we must isolate ourselves to avoid risking exposure and rejection.

The truth, however, is that we are designed in the image of a holy God, who embodies community and who invites us into His family. We are created for community.

LIE: I can solve my own problems.

TRUTH: God made me to live known and loved.

> If we walk in the light, as he is in the light, we have
> fellowship with one another, and the blood of
> Jesus his Son cleanses us from all sin.[3]

I CHOOSE TO BE KNOWN.

We Have a Choice

EMOTION
SHAME

THOUGHT
I CAN SOLVE
MY OWN PROBLEMS

BEHAVIOR
BUILD WALLS

RELATIONSHIPS
ISOLATED

CONSEQUENCE
LONELY

CONSEQUENCE
KNOWN

RELATIONSHIPS
CONNECTED

BEHAVIOR
BUILD BRIDGES

THOUGHT
GOD MADE ME
TO LIVE KNOWN
AND LOVED

I CHOOSE TO BE KNOWN

EMOTION
SHAME

Hardwired to Connect

Our bodies are hardwired for connection with others. Have you ever heard of mirror neurons? When you are sitting across from a friend at coffee, both of your mirror neuron systems are firing. These neurons are at work when your friend smiles, letting you experience the feeling associated with smiling.

Mirror neurons help you feel what the other is feeling. In this way, empathy is hardly a contrived response but rather an automatic response our bodies have to each other. One researcher goes so far as to say that there is, in fact, no such thing as nonconformity, writing that "the self is more of a superhighway for social influence than it is the impenetrable private fortress we believe it to be."[4]

And while you and I recognize many of the ways interpersonal connection has influenced us from infancy to this moment—one licensed counselor called early caregiver responses "brain food" for the developing mind[5]—what may not be as obvious are the ways that *disconnection* alters our brains.

The part of your brain that activates when you feel rejected or uninvited by a friend is the same part of your brain that fires when you're in physical pain.[6] Maybe this is why breakups and severed friendships literally hurt.

When you and I isolate, we switch into self-preservation mode. We may respond more harshly to a friend who says the wrong thing at the wrong time or get defensive when a coworker gently critiques our project. Loneliness can make us think that everything is a threat, even if there is no real threat to be found.

Loneliness has been linked to heart disease.
And depression.

And chronic stress.
And poor sleep.[7]

If we want to approach life fully in the way that Jesus Himself modeled, then we will do life together instead of choosing to go it alone. We weren't made to celebrate victory alone. We weren't made to suffer hardship alone. We weren't made to walk through the dailiness of life alone. We weren't made to be alone with our thoughts. (Are you as happy as I am about that last one? What a terrifying place the mind can be.) We were made to reach out, to connect, to stay tethered. We were made to live together in the light.

The apostle Paul beautifully described this way of living:

If there is any encouragement in Christ, any comfort from love, any participation in the Spirit, any affection and sympathy, complete my joy by being of the same mind, having the same love, being in full accord and of one mind.[8]

He gave us clear direction on what this looks like in our interactions:

Put on then, as God's chosen ones, holy and beloved, compassionate hearts, kindness, humility, meekness, and patience, bearing with one another and, if one has a complaint against another, forgiving each other; as the Lord has forgiven you, so you also must forgive. And above all these put on love, which binds everything together in perfect harmony. And let the peace of Christ rule in your hearts, to which indeed you were called in one body. And be thankful. Let the word of Christ dwell in you richly, teaching and admonishing one another in all wisdom, singing psalms and hymns and spiritual songs, with thankfulness in your hearts to God.[9]

It's a lot of togetherness, right?

Several of my friends are counselors or therapists, and they all have confirmed the same thing: the prevalence of group therapy is on the rise because it *works,* even when little else does. **It is not just comforting to have someone else in our corner; it's scientifically proven to *heal.*** [10]

While studying the effects of stress on female behavior, UCLA researchers found that women seek out more social support during times of stress than men do. Other research has shown that having a strong social network can help people stay healthy. [11]

Yep. A tribe, a posse, a squad changes us even physically. We were built by a communal God for community. We need this!

We need this, friend.

BETTER TOGETHER

God purposefully places us in community so that our friends can help us in the battle for our thought lives. When our mind maps are chaotic, our thoughts are spiraling, and our emotions are running the show, so often our escape plan involves simply reaching out, just whispering that little word "Help."

You and I need to be able to seek out wisdom and insight when our own brains can't sort out the answers, can't muster the willpower, can't find the strength, can't remember how to pray. Relationships like that take time, effort, and energy to cultivate, but they shift everything.

I can look back over the course of my life and see how my closest girlfriends at each age and stage protected me from lesser dreams. My darling baby sisters, my grade-school recess buddies, my high school friends, the other cheerleaders at Arkansas, the girls who came to my first Bible studies, my Austin people, my church small group in Dallas—each community has shaped me, helped me feel known, made me run further and faster than I thought I could. Hopefully I've done the same for them. Yes,

I CHOOSE COMMUNITY

we've fought. Yes, we've grown apart. Yes, we've hurt one another at times. This is all part of the deal. But the strongest bonds get forged through difficulty.

It's true that choosing community over isolation can be downright scary. It requires us to take a risk.

Researcher and author Brené Brown said, "Vulnerability is the core, the heart, the center, of meaningful human experiences."[12] Or put another way: **we must be known in order to be healthy.**[13]

Isn't that a profound perspective? Tell me the people who know you and how deep that knowledge runs, and I will tell you how healthy you are.[14]

Gulp.

Some people would look at my track record over the years and say, "Clearly, Jennie, you've got nothing to worry about. You've *always* let people in." Maybe. But I have to tell you, when our family recently moved to Dallas after living for ten years in Austin, building a new and trusted circle was no small concern. How could I make "old friends" fast?

Displacement from a long-standing network of support is a challenge to living in meaningful community, but it's hardly the only one. The more people I encounter, the more valid reasons I hear for why community "just isn't for me." I think of a young woman who lives in a town so small that there was outright celebration last year when they got their first traffic light. "Jennie, there is nobody for me to connect with," she told me. "I'm not sure another woman in her twenties even *exists* in my hometown."

Or how about the women I've met who are full-on introverts? For them, signing up for this community thing sounds like a stressful and exhausting proposition.

I understand that maybe you've suffered a painful betrayal—or more than one—and that keeps you from engaging now. You have risked trusting someone with your struggle, and that decision has come back to bite you in the rear. "Not doing that again," you say. I get it!

Then there's the matter of upkeep. Once you *do* share your struggle with another person, you feel obligated to keep that person apprised of any progress or setbacks you face.

And here's another thing: we can't control how people will respond once we've let them in on our struggles. They might say something insensitive. They might minimize the depth of our pain. They might paste on a smile and quote Scripture at us. They might do *all* these things on the same day.

To these and a thousand other pushbacks, I have only one response: *you're right.*

You're right.

You are!

But every valuable relationship in my life is one I have had to fight for.

People can be jerks and flighty, inconsiderate and self-centered and forgetful. I know this because I am a person, and I've been all these things at some point. Also true: you are a person too.

So instead of letting the enemy hold us captive in isolation, let's remind ourselves of this truth: I have a choice. I can remember that the Spirit of God lives inside me and He will walk with me as I reach out to others who are just as human and just as in need of connection and grace as I am.

When I started IF, a misunderstanding ensued regarding my ministry motivations and gained a lot of attention on social media. Many women I admire and strive to emulate took offense, believing that I really did have malicious intent. It felt as if battle lines quickly got drawn, dividing all my heroes and me. It was a humbling, sobering experience that left me staggering in disbelief.

Not knowing what else to do, I began placing phone calls to each of those women. I apologized for my part in the misunderstanding. I requested wisdom regarding how to make things right going forward. I blessed them for their influence on my life.

Thankfully, not only did they each take my call, but they worked toward unity too. We sorted out a way forward, and I count them as some of my dearest friends still today. But following that experience, I was skittish relationally. I was afraid of saying or doing *anything* that might leave me ostracized again. But I finally decided I couldn't keep stepping hesitantly into relationships.

Nobody can play defense forever; we have to show up. With our whole selves.

When I come to a moment when I am staring at the risk of showing up in my friendships, I choose to show up. And then when stuff happens (because it will), we work through it. But you know what? When we are faithful to keep showing up for our lives, those lives make room for us.

I met a new friend after the move to Dallas. Ellen is sophisticated and always says the right thing. She files every piece of mail she gets. I don't even open my mail! We had mutual friends who suggested our families join a small group together. I tell her this now, but she was the kind of new friend who is so awesome, you feel intimidated around her (though she would never want you to). The first time we met, I remember playing it safe. I thought I'd hold back and feel her out.

But the second time, I decided to go for it. I was all of me—opinionated, loud, honest, and passionate. She laughed and started calling more often. She wasn't wanting to be friends with someone just like her. She liked me in all my chaotic glory. Now, plenty of other relational risks I've taken have not turned out that way, but that's how we find our people.

GATHER YOUR TEAM

As we make this choice to stop trying to do life on our own and instead risk in the context of other real live human beings, we must have two resources at our disposal: both the *awareness* to know what we need and the *courageous gumption* to go out and get it.

Here are a few encouragements that may push you out of your comfort zone and help you find your people.

Seek Out Healthy People

Here is Paul's advice on the subject: "Follow my example, as I follow the example of Christ."[15]

Follow me, as I follow Christ. If you want to know whom to connect with in community, look for someone whose life shouts those words. Find someone who is following *hard* after Jesus, and then ask that person to coffee.

In the past year, I have found that by seeking out healthy people in Dallas, I've been made healthier too. Even the process of looking for whole friendships has ushered in more wholeness for me. Now, notice I didn't say to seek out *perfect* people. *Whole* people. *Healthy* people.

Does this potential friend of yours seem to be in touch with her strengths and weaknesses? Is she clear on the values that guide her life? When she feels all the feels, is she then able to kind of rein it in? Is she thriving in other relationships, or does she seem closed off from the world? Do you feel seen and valued when you interact with her? Does she listen well, or is she always turning the conversation back to herself? Is she motivated to grow? Does she seem happy? Is she at peace?

Again, nobody is going to get this stuff right 100 percent of the time. What I'm asking you to look for is a pattern of progress here. When you're looking for intimate friendships, you've got to start with emotionally intelligent friends.

And guess what? We have to become those emotionally healthy friends too! If no one ever wants to be friends with you, there might be reasons. Are you growing in health and not bitterness? I am a big fan of counseling because it can disrupt unhealthy patterns we barely notice in ourselves.

Just Ask

When you find someone you want to get to know better, *just ask* whether she'd like to connect. "Do you want to get a cup of coffee tomorrow afternoon?" "Have you ever checked out the hiking trail up behind our neighborhood?" "Do you and your husband like to play board games?" "Would you like to meet up for dinner before Bible study next week?"

See how straightforward this is?

Several months ago, I realized that despite the level of social intelligence and genuine desire for community and earnest transparency exhibited by the young women who work with me day in and day out at IF, there were still way too many occasions when they weren't comfortable asking for help.

During staff meeting one Tuesday, this subject came up, and I took the liberty of asking, "How many of you feel awkward asking for help, even when you really, really need some help?"

Every arm shot up.

Wow.

"Girls," I said. "For *real*. We have to get this addressed."

We talked for a while about what was making them uncomfortable, and then I issued a collective task: at least one time over the following twenty-four hours, each of them had to ask for help.

Ask for creative input, I told them.

Ask for help unloading your car.

Ask for an afternoon walk.

Ask for advice about a problem.

I didn't care what they asked for; I just wanted them to practice asking.

Ask until asking no longer makes you cringe. That advice might just save your life someday, so I'll repeat it for you here: *ask until asking no longer makes you cringe.*

Ask, and ask, and ask.

Say Yes

Now, I'm someone who regards novelty as oxygen, so this one is easy for me. But even if you're an introverted homebody, you can do this: *every so often, say yes.* Only one caveat here: this doesn't mean we open the floodgates to toxic, unhealthy people. We say yes to real, healthy friendships.[16]

A few weeks ago, my darling Austin-based friend Jessica reached out to tell me that her birthday was fast approaching and she wanted to spend time together. "Will you come?" she asked. (She is a fantastic asker!) "Pleeeease?"

Did I mention that her birthday was the following week and that getting together meant traveling three-plus hours?

Was the timing of this little excursion convenient? It was not.

Was it worth it? It absolutely was.

As I say, I might push the just-say-yes envelope too far, far too much of the time. But here's the thing to remember: *if you never, ever say yes to an invitation, those invitations will cease to exist.*

Doing life together helps us right our wrong thinking. But we can do life together only if we're actually *together* from time to time.

"Yes! I'd love to join you."

"Yes! I'd be happy to go."

"Yes! Let's set a phone date."

If somewhere along the way you've become a decliner, one who declines every invitation that comes your way, then just for today, might you try on a *yes* for size?

Be All of You, Fast

Our spiraling thoughts of isolation threaten to keep us trapped in a place of self-sufficiency and shame, but vulnerability brings those to a screeching halt. So, be *all* of you right away, so that your friends get you—the *real* you.

I can be obnoxious and I'm the first to admit it. I laugh at inappropriate times, like in court and at funerals and during my child's performance of the speech she worked hard on. (Why do I do this? Can someone tell me, please?) I ask intense, intrusive questions. I'm forgetful. I interrupt serious moments to ask where you got your cute sweater. I flit around in conversation like a hummingbird, incapable of seeing a subject through to its logical end.

And just like with my friend Ellen, relationally my choices are two: Either I can "class it up" when I meet new people and pretend to be something I'm not. Or I can relish my wholehearted mess of a self with a good bit of self-deprecation and laughter and be at peace, just being me with them.

In such brave endeavors, we may scare off the wrong people sooner but we'll bring in the right people more quickly too.

Bother Others, and Let Others Bother You

As acquaintances deepen and broaden into friendships, the asks can feel tougher. The stakes are higher now, and fear of rejection is a real thing. My counsel: *go for broke.* When you notice that your friend isn't herself, bug her until she shoots straight. Invite her to tea. Invite her to lunch. Tell her you want to pray for her because you know something is drastically wrong. Bother her until she feels safe enough to vent. She'll thank you for that bothering someday.

Likewise, to experience true community, you've got to be botherable yourself. Take the risk to trust someone with the truth of your life today. Yes, you might get hurt. Yes, you might feel embarrassed. Yes, it might be uncomfortable. But better the discomfort of a friend holding your hand and your truth than the discomfort of thinking you're alone.

Before we move on, let me make sure you noticed the order of the two parts of this last rule: First, you take the initiative. And then, you let others take the initiative with you. I can't help but notice that every time I post on Instagram about friendship and the value of doing life in community, I get responses such as these:

"No one wants to be my friend."

"No one ever reaches out."

"I do my part, but no one ever reciprocates."

"Nobody cares about me."

Listen—giving thoughts such as these space in your mind and heart is giving the enemy a free pass. These things just are not true! The irony here is that many of the people you think don't care about you are feeling the very same way. They are worried that if they put themselves out there, they will be rejected. They are frustrated that nobody seems to be reciprocating the care they extend. They are wondering if anyone wants to be friends with them.

Which is why I'm begging you: Go be the botherer first. Reach out. Take the risk. Say what you're feeling. Listen well. **Be the friend you wish others would be for you.**[17]

A while back my daughter Kate was out of town with her friend and her friend's family, and when she called me to check in, I could tell by the sound of her voice that something was bugging her, that something was off. She'd been that way for a few days, so I took a risk and probed.

Kate didn't offer much information but did ask whether it would be okay with Zac and me if she talked with a counselor once she was back. Zac and I are wholehearted believers in the usefulness of counseling, believing that we *all* need "translators" from time to time to reflect back to us what we're thinking and how we're feeling, that we *all* need to hear the truth about ourselves in a safe environment, that we *all* need space to sort out our deeper needs, and that we *all* need help applying God's Word to the realities of our lives. In short, this was an easy *yes*. "But before you book an appointment," I said to Kate, "I want you to know you can always try me."

I told Kate that there was nothing I wouldn't have grace for and that there was nothing that could impact my love for her. It took a lot of time and used up a lot of tears, but two hours later, when I was still on the phone with my incredible daughter, I felt more grateful for the power of community than I have in a long, long time.

I found a greeting card at a café in Colorado Springs one time that featured a sketch of a lovable-looking bear with the words "We were together. I forget the rest." That's how I'll always feel about that monumental phone chat with Kate. The details of what was bugging her have already faded with time, but that feeling of togetherness has not and will not. She was determined to tell *someone* who could help her.

I was so grateful it got to be me.

The Last 2 Percent

If we want to be free of the chaos, friend, we cannot stay alone in the dark with the devil. We need to be rescuers, and we need to choose to gather a team around us.

I have a choice. I can be known!

Let me tell you what is on the line and the beautiful thing that happens when we let one another in.

We have this saying at my home church in Dallas: "Say the last 2 percent." Maybe you think you have learned the secret of mastering authenticity. You'll mention your struggle with a sin or a fear or an insecurity, but even those of us who value authenticity often have one card that we don't put down.

It's the little secret we won't show our families. It's the one we won't share with our friends. It's a card we don't play. Maybe your 2 percent is that you felt rage at your young children today. Or maybe it is a mistake you made years ago that you have never told anyone about. Let me tell you what it was for one of my friends.

Jennifer leads Bible studies in her home in Austin. She and her husband are leaders in their church. They're an incredible couple. They love Jesus, and she's one of my favorite friends.

So real. I like her so much because she often is vulnerable with me. But recently she called to share something she'd been holding back.

She told me that over the course of the last semester, she had been attracted to her coworker. At first it was subtle. "He was cute, but I don't know how it happened. I love my husband, and I value our marriage," she said, "but I found myself attracted to him." She began lingering after meetings. Then she said, "I know this is crazy, and I hope you won't think less of me, but I started texting with him."

Then she told me, "At IF:Gathering I pulled our mutual friend aside and said, 'I need to lay down the last 2 percent I am not sharing with anyone. I need to say it.'" Then she said it out loud.

And here's where it gets crazy. She said, "Jennie, the moment I said it out loud, I have never been attracted to him since."[18]

Yeah, it's crazy.

We have stayed in the dark with the devil, and we have kept our secrets close. We don't show anyone all our cards. Why would we? We think, *It's not that big of a deal. It doesn't mean anything. And I'm not going to do it again anyway.*

We don't play our last cards, and the devil has us in our secrets.

But when we say out loud what's in our thoughts, when we reveal our dark struggles, we take them captive and break their power. We test the gospel and allow it to stand. We bring in community. This is how God created us to fight!

Seen. Known. Loved.

Let's fight for this!

What if my worst nightmare comes true?

They probably think I'm . . .

I'm not good enough for this.

Did I say that the wrong way?

What will happen to me if . . .

Everything is out of control.

I'm so inadequate at my job, he's
probably going to fire me any minute.

Something horrible is going to happen to them.

Unafraid

I Choose to Surrender My Fears to God

MY CHEST WAS SO TIGHT, I COULDN'T BREATHE. IT WAS a Sunday night before a busy week, and I was excited about everything ahead of me.

Why couldn't I catch a breath?

I sat in my bed because I didn't know where else to be. It was as if my body were yelling "Something is wrong!" and my mind was racing to figure out what it was.

I've noticed that sometimes our minds seem to lag behind our emotions, while our bodies are right in sync, sending us cues that something internal is happening. In fact, I think it is a gift that God built our bodies to send us signals that we might be spiraling in a dangerous direction.

I was in the middle of writing this book, and I sensed God using this moment of spiraling confusion to remind me that taking every thought captive isn't merely a helpful process to adopt. *Don't forget, Jennie, this is all-out war.*

Zac sat next to me as I wrapped my arms around my middle, as if holding myself together. When I half-jokingly bribed him to bum a Xanax off our neighbors, he lovingly informed me, "That would be illegal, baby."

So I sat still. I prayed. And I searched my mind for what my body was telling me was wrong.

Sure enough, as I started digging into the crevices of recent patterns of thinking, I noticed something.

Yes, I was excited about the awesome opportunities for ministry in the coming weeks. But a subtle lie had begun to overshadow them all. These subtle lies can feel like a heavy coat we unconsciously slip into, perhaps out of habit, on a perfectly warm sunny day.

The spiral I had entered into was this: *What if I fail? What if I am not enough for this work?*

Adding weight to all that was the familiar whisper from the dark: *I am worthless.*

I'd been walking around with this vague, undefined heaviness. If it had been a conscious thought, I would have immediately fought it and chosen the truth: *God is enough for me. God chooses the least qualified so He gets the glory. I don't have to measure up.*

But I hadn't even noticed what was happening until the lie pulled me into a spiral and my body revealed the anxiety that had set me spinning.

WORRIED ABOUT MANY THINGS

How many of us are dragging through our days, weighed down by anxiety? Many of us find our thoughts circling around problematic circumstances or people. For others of us, anxiety has become the soundtrack of our days, so familiar we hardly notice it playing in the background of every scene. (Please know that I'm talking here about thought patterns, not about anxiety that is rooted in our bodies' chemistry and for which I urge you to seek professional help, if this is your situation.)

The enemy has ensnared us with two little words: "What if?" With those two little words, he sets our imaginations whirling, spinning tales of the doom that lurks ahead.

But our tool for defeating "what if" is, not surprisingly, found in two words: "Because God."

Because God clothes the lilies of the field and feeds the birds of the air, we don't need to be anxious about tomorrow.[1]

Because God has poured His love into our hearts, our hope will not be put to shame.[2]

Because God chose us to be saved by His strength, we can stand firm in our faith no matter what the day holds.[3]

Freedom begins when we notice what it is that is binding us. Then we can interrupt it with the truth.

Anxiety says, "What if?"

- *What if I get too close to this person and she manipulates me like the last friend I trusted?*
- *What if my spouse cheats on me?*
- *What if my children die tragically?*
- *What if my boss decides I'm expendable?*
- *What if . . .*
- *What if . . .*

Certainly there are healthy levels of anxiety that signal our brains to be afraid of things that are truly worth being afraid of—like a bear in the woods or oncoming traffic when we cross a street.

As an editor for *Medical News Today* noted, "It is when this life-saving mechanism is triggered at inappropriate times or gets stuck in the 'on' position that it becomes a problem."[4] The type of anxiety that sends our thoughts spiraling is when our emotional reaction to scary things goes beyond rational to illogical because our brains' fear networks are in overdrive.

We keep finding new concerns to worry about and new facets to each concern, as if by constant stewing we can prepare ourselves for what's to come. We experience palpable physical responses to things that are not real threats, and our future-tense fears are leaving us bound up with tight chests, unable to relax or be present, utterly forgetting that there is a God who will give us what we need today, next week, and twenty years from now, even if our very worst nightmares come true.

We are "what-iffing" ourselves to death.

But there is a better way, because we have a choice.

LIE: I cannot trust God to take care of my tomorrows.

TRUTH: God is in control of every day of my life.

> The very hairs on your head are all numbered. So
> don't be afraid; you are more valuable to God
> than a whole flock of sparrows.[5]

I CHOOSE TO SURRENDER MY FEARS TO GOD.

We Have a Choice

EMOTION
FEAR OF REAL OR
PERCEIVED THREAT

THOUGHT
I CANNOT TRUST GOD
TO TAKE CARE OF
MY TOMORROWS

BEHAVIOR
RESISTANT TO
GOD'S AUTHORITY

RELATIONSHIPS
CONTROLLING AND
MANIPULATIVE

CONSEQUENCE
CONSTANT ANXIETY

CONSEQUENCE
UNAFRAID

RELATIONSHIPS
PRESENT
AND OPEN

BEHAVIOR
SUBMITTED TO
GOD'S AUTHORITY

THOUGHT
GOD IS IN CONTROL OF
EVERY DAY OF MY LIFE

I CHOOSE TO SURRENDER

EMOTION
FEAR OF REAL OR
PERCEIVED THREAT

What Is Real

Paul knew we would spiral, so he told us to replace the lies with something surprising. In Philippians 4, he wrote,

> Do not be anxious about anything, but in every situation, by prayer and petition, with thanksgiving, present your requests to God. And the peace of God, which transcends all understanding, will guard your hearts and your minds in Christ Jesus.
>
> Finally, brothers and sisters, whatever is true, whatever is noble, whatever is right, whatever is pure, whatever is lovely, whatever is admirable—if anything is excellent or praiseworthy—think about such things.[6]

First I want you to see what he called us to. It's not just a suggestion but a clear instruction: "Do not be anxious about anything."

Anything?

Anything.

How could Paul say that? Does God really command this of us?

Well, Paul had plenty to be anxious about. When he wrote those words, you may remember, he was locked in prison with a death sentence on his head. Paul meant what he wrote. He meant it for one simple reason: this earth is not our home, and our home in heaven is secure. So if death is not to be feared, what exactly do we have to be scared of?

God's promises give us ultimate hope in absolutely every circumstance. He meets every need. He will resolve (in the end) every problem we may face here on earth. Paul wrote confidently of this truth, and then he gave us clear guidance for ridding ourselves of anxious thoughts:

1. Choose to be grateful.
2. Choose to think about what is true, noble, right, pure, lovely, admirable, excellent, and praiseworthy.

For just a moment, let's zero in on one of these replacement thoughts: "Whatever is true . . . think about such things."

What gets most of us in trouble isn't even real fears. We worry about things that may never happen. In fact, research shows that "97 percent of what you worry over is not much more than a fearful mind punishing you with exaggerations and misperceptions."[7]

My sister Katie is a 6 on the Enneagram, a modern personality-typing system with centuries-old roots, and she constantly cracks me up because about 50 percent of our conversations center on hypothetical scenarios. On the Enneagram I am a 7. What this means for Katie and me is that while she is forever figuring out how things could go wrong, I'm fixated on all that could go *right*.

I daresay it's easier for someone of my type to follow Paul's instructions here; still, regardless of personality, **God has called us to hope, to joy, to perseverance—to think on what is true!**

In the gospel of John, we find an incredible description of the enemy. Jesus was frustrated because there were all kinds of confusion around what He was doing and why. He said to those arguing against Him,

> If God were your Father, you would love me, for I came from God and I am here. I came not of my own accord, but he sent me. Why do you not understand what I say? It is because you cannot bear to hear my word. You are of your father the devil, and your will is to

do your father's desires. He was a murderer from the beginning, and does not stand in the truth, because there is no truth in him. When he lies, he speaks out of his own character, for he is a liar and the father of lies.[8]

Truth is the most powerful weapon we have against the enemy, who is "a liar and the father of lies." So we fight the enemy with whatever is true—meaning, whatever is real!

Take a look at the tool on the facing page.

Take one of the anxious thoughts you have running around in that head of yours and write it down.

So what is the thought?

Now diagnose the thought. Is it true?

Take it one step further and consider, What does God say about this thought? To answer that question, you consult Scripture and you do that with trusted people in your community. You say, "Here's this thought, and what does God say about it? What is the truth?"

Then you have to make a choice: Will you believe God or believe the lie?

I think most of us are probably good at finding the thought, recognizing it as a lie, and even knowing what the truth is. But we fail on the last step. We keep believing the lie, acting on it, letting the "what ifs" stir our thoughts into a frenzy.

What I realized, in emerging from my eighteen-month spiral of doubt, was that I had to go to war. I had to read God's Word and find every weapon available to fight it.

Don't you know that Paul had to do this while imprisoned? He had to fight for belief. "To me, to live is Christ and to die is gain. If I am to go on living in the body, this will mean fruitful labor for me. Yet what shall I choose? I do not know!"[9]

GRAB THE THOUGHT
What is it?

DIAGNOSE THE THOUGHT
Is it true?

TAKE IT TO GOD
What does God
say about it?

MAKE A CHOICE
Am I going to
believe God?

Yes, faith is a gift, but it is a hard-won gift at times. Paul wrote honestly of how God met him in his struggle: "He said to me, 'My grace is sufficient for you, for my power is made perfect in weakness.' Therefore I will boast all the more gladly about my weaknesses, so that Christ's power may rest on me."[10]

I was deeply comforted by that. It reassured me that my own fight for faith is a work in progress.

I can keep teaching the Bible, I can continue to lead IF, and I can continue to take my kids to church, because God is real. My feelings are based largely not on what is real but on made-up narratives in my head.

What *is* real?

God is real. He is not going anywhere, even if my mind jumps to all kinds of dark places. I can't rely on my thoughts or feelings to hold my faith in place. God holds my faith in place.

But What Do I Do?

The woman standing before me was reeling with anxiety. Her teenage daughter was making some seriously poor decisions in life, and this mama's heart was breaking into a thousand pieces. With tears in her eyes, she looked at me and asked, "Jennie, what do I do?"

What do I do?

I've heard countless women ask this question, women facing all sorts of challenges—cheating husbands and debilitating addictions and failed financial ventures and wayward kids and devastating diagnoses and . . . and . . . and . . .

Each time, after they explain what has been trying their patience and tempting their hearts and tripping them up, they ask that same question: "What do I do?"

I CHOOSE TO TRUST GOD →

What they're wondering is what they should do to fix the situation. Or to fix their perspective. Or to keep pain and suffering at bay.

Or if none of those things are a possibility, they want me to tell them how in the world they keep moving forward without giving in to desperation and despair.

What do we do? We confront our thoughts. We tear down strongholds by the power of God. We figure out if we are believing something untrue or unreal about God or ourselves, and we go to battle there.

Psst. Let me tell you the greatest news: You are not God. You are not omniscient.

When we allow our thoughts to spin out of control with worry and fear, either consciously or unconsciously, we try to elbow our way into the all-knowing role that only God can play. We forget that it's actually good news that He is in control and we are not. You and I may have many gifts and talents, but being God is not one of them.

Now, this is easier preached and harder lived, but that's why we are going to stick together and steep in God's Word. Change is difficult and may come slowly. After all, our fears arise from ingrained thoughts and entangled sins. But because we have been made new creations, we have the Spirit's power to make the choice for truth.

Changing our minds *is* possible.

When you recognize the lie resting heavily on your shoulders, you can take off that suffocating coat and set it aside.

What fear-filled thought is Satan using to suffocate your faith?
Name it.
Say its name.

- *I'm afraid that I won't be able to withstand whatever the future might hold.*

    I choose to believe God will not allow me to be tempted beyond what I can endure and will always give me the strength to overcome temptation.[11]

- *I'm afraid that everyone will abandon me.*

    I choose to believe God has promised not to leave me, and He always keeps His promises.[12]

- *I'm afraid of losing everything and everyone I love.*

    I choose to believe God will sustain me in my brightest moments of victory and my darkest moments of suffering.[13]

- *I'm afraid of being found out.*

    I choose to believe God knows every thought before I think it and loves me.[14]

- *I'm afraid that I'm really not capable of doing this job.*

    I choose to believe God has given me everything I need to live a godly life.[15]

- *I'm afraid of being rejected.*

    I choose to believe God has accepted me as His child and will never leave me.[16]

- *I'm afraid of not living up to their expectations.*

    I choose to believe God wants me to seek His approval only and release the pressure to please people.[17]

- *I'm afraid of failing miserably for everyone to see.*

    I choose to believe God specializes in taking weakness and using it for His glory.[18]

This is how we fight the spiral. We pull the thoughts out of our heads, and we steal all their power and then replace them with what is true!

ANXIOUS FOR NOTHING

My friend Jackie has tried to get pregnant for five years. The ache in her soul has been nearly unbearable. I was with her not long ago, and her despair had grown so intense that she was losing all hope in life, in God, in His "good and perfect gift[s]."[19]

She looked at me as if to say, "What if He passes over me? What if my dreams don't come true?"

As we talked, with a whole herd of people she loved surrounding her, woman after woman loaned Jackie her faith. They weren't believing God on Jackie's behalf for a child to show up in her womb; they were believing God on Jackie's behalf, *regardless of what may come.*

She left our time together glowing and hopeful, eyes set on trying some new challenges and embracing a world that may not contain a child in her womb. Because God is good and perfect, even when life is not—and she is choosing to believe He is in control.

There are no promises that our worst fears won't come true. Sometimes they do, but even then God remains our unfailing hope.

Cancer can come against us, yet by God's power, it will not win, at least not in the end.

A spouse may be unfaithful, yet by God's power, infidelity won't define our lives.

Financial crisis can come against us, yet by God's power, we can move forward.

Disillusionment and doubt can come against us, yet by God's power, they won't have the last word.

My sister-in-law, Ashley, reads Corrie ten Boom's book *The Hiding Place* every year. She says it reminds her that, no matter what the coming months hold for her and her family, God is enough.

Recently, as I confided in her some of my fears about one of my kids, she reminded me of this story Corrie told in the book:

Father sat down on the edge of the narrow bed. "Corrie," he began gently, "when you and I go to Amsterdam—when do I give you your ticket?"

I sniffed a few times, considering this.

"Why, just before we get on the train."

"Exactly. And our wise Father in heaven knows when we're going to need things, too. Don't run out ahead of Him, Corrie. When the time comes that some of us will have to die, you will look into your heart and find the strength you need—just in time."[20]

We always have exactly what we need, when we need it. Do we believe that?

If we believe we have a choice to trust instead of fear, then how will choosing to trust cause us to live?

We will live in what is true of us, which is that we have the mind of Christ.

Paul declared this to be true in Philippians 2:5: "Have this mind among yourselves, which is yours in Christ Jesus"!

So what do we do when we start to spin?

We do the work.

We risk telling someone, even if what we're worrying about sounds silly.

We actively choose to close the curtain on fearful, untrue thoughts.

We remind ourselves who God is, and we cast our anxieties on Him.[21] You may have to do this a hundred times a day.

And we claim the peace of God as our promise.

After my recent Sunday evening bout with anxiety, I "phoned a friend." Callie listened as I said it all, even that last 2 percent that made me feel ashamed. And then she laughed a little and said, "Okay, Jennie. That is a lie from the devil. And you are not going to let this paralyze you anymore!"

She fought for me, and when I couldn't pull myself out, she lifted me out.

Friend, I want to do the same for you. Please hear me: no matter how your life looks today, no matter what tomorrow holds, God does care for us.

> Consider the lilies, how they grow: they neither toil nor spin, yet I tell you, even Solomon in all his glory was not arrayed like one of these. But if God so clothes the grass, which is alive in the field today, and tomorrow is thrown into the oven, how much more will he clothe you, O you of little faith![22]

O we of little faith. We are seen and cared for, and there is nothing to fear because God has us.

If I don't look out for myself, who will?

Nothing is as good as it seems.

If I've learned anything, it's that you
should never trust what people say.

If I don't keep my guard up,
I'll get taken advantage of.

Don't get your hopes up. You'll just
be setting yourself up for a fall.

Belief is for fools.

I'm fine. I don't need help from
anything or anyone.

A Beautiful Interruption

I Choose to Delight in God

MY TEAM FROM IF:GATHERING AND I EAT TEX-MEX together a lot. Recently, we were at Matt's El Rancho, eating queso and discussing optimism. I had been studying the subject and thinking that we all—both as individuals and as a team—needed more of it. My IF:Gathering team feels more like the best of war buddies than office mates. We have been through a few battles together.

That afternoon at Matt's, we were talking specifically about the opposite of optimism: cynicism. My research into negative thinking had confirmed that, as with all spiral thought patterns, we always have a choice. We may not choose the situations and the people in our lives, but we can choose how we react. We get to choose how our minds, and therefore our lives, will go.

Here is the analogy I shared with them to try to make my point.

If we went together to a party one evening and the people we sat next to were complaining about the tasteless food, the lame playlist, and the rude hosts, we'd come away with the impression that the party had been a bad experience. Truth be told, we might not have minded the food or the environment, but those gripes would sway us to that negative side.

We would walk away thinking, *That was a terrible party.*

But if we went to the same party and instead sat next to people who were raving about the delicious food, the energetic music, the thoughtful seating, and the kind and generous hosts, we would leave saying, "What a fun party!"

What if instead of a party we were talking about our lives? How often have we *chosen* to be unhappy? Rather than seeing the best and celebrating the good, we have chosen to see only the struggles and complain about the bad.

I wondered aloud how choosing to see the best in all situations might bring all of us a lot more joy.

One of my colleagues commented, "Jennie, I hear you. But if I choose to see the best in life, I am going to get taken advantage of." Others affirmed her perspective. They were a little worried that if they didn't keep their guard up, people would see their naivete and they would be targeted.

That's fair, I thought.

I'll never forget what Elizabeth, another of our team, then said, "So what? Wouldn't you be happier?"

Elizabeth is made of sunshine and sweetness, always smiling, always kind; of *course* she'd say something like this. Yet something about her response rang true. She was right: the alternative to a life unguarded is self-preservation and debilitating pessimism.

Who wants to live that way?

THE TRANSFORMING POWER OF AWE

Cynicism has become esteemed in our culture, as if we've concluded the cynics know something the rest of us don't. They are prepared and guarded and *aware* at a level that the rest of us are too flighty to grasp. But at its core, cynicism isn't so wonderful. In fact, it's not wonderful at all.

Cynicism is *always* driven by fear of the future or by anger regarding the past. Either we're afraid of something that might not ever occur, or we project something that *has* occurred onto all the days that are to come. We buy into the lie that it's too risky to be vulnerable or hope for good things.

Brené Brown calls this foreboding joy. "Scarcity and fear drive foreboding joy," she wrote in her book *Daring Greatly.*

> We're afraid that the feeling of joy won't last, or that there won't be
> enough, or that the transition to disappointment (or whatever is in
> store for us next) will be too difficult. We've learned that giving in
> to joy is, at best, setting ourselves up for disappointment and, at
> worst, inviting disaster.[1]

The enemy's strategy is to flood our thoughts with visions of all that is wrong in this broken, fallen world to the point we don't even think to look for the positive anymore. Cynicism just becomes the way we think, and we don't even notice.

Here are some questions to ask yourself to see whether cynicism has invaded your headspace:

- Do you get annoyed when people are optimistic?
- When someone is nice to you, do you wonder what that person wants?
- Do you constantly feel misunderstood?
- When things are going well, are you waiting for the bottom to fall out?
- Do you quickly notice people's flaws?
- Do you worry about getting taken advantage of?
- Are you guarded when you meet someone new?

- Do you wonder why people just can't get it together?
- Are you often sarcastic?

Cynicism is destroying our ability to delight in the world around us and fully engage with others. God has an abundance of joy and delight for us, and we're missing it with arms crossed. What if there was another way to live?

When researchers studied awe and beauty, they found an interesting connection: when we experience awe, we move toward others in beneficial ways.

When we are overcome by the grandeur of a snowy mountain peak or delighted by a beautiful song, when we sit silently in an old church and marvel at the way the sunlight seeps through the stained-glass windows, or when we're delighted by our children's squeals as they run through the sprinkler in the backyard, we let go of our "it's all about me" fixation. We are freed from being the center of our own worlds for just a moment, and in doing so, we become more invested in the well-being of others, more generous, less entitled.[2]

Have you experienced this? It's the moment when your heart swells and feels as if it might explode trying to take in how beautiful something is.

Cynicism says, "I'm surrounded by incompetence, fraudsters, and disappointment."

Delight in God and His goodness tears down our walls and allows hope, trust, and worship to flood in.

And guess how worship springs up in us? When we look to the source of all delight—God Himself—instead of our temporary problems.

Consider Paul's description of what happens when we, like the Israel-ites, turn our gaze away from the things that fade and look to the eternal God:

> Whenever, though, they turn to face God as Moses did, God removes the veil and there they are—face-to-face! They suddenly recognize that God is a living, personal presence, not a piece of chiseled stone. And when God is personally present, a living Spirit, that old, constricting legislation is recognized as obsolete. We're free of it! All of us! Nothing between us and God, our faces shining with the brightness of his face. And so we are transfigured much like the Messiah, our lives gradually becoming brighter and more beautiful as God enters our lives and we become like him.[3]

Just as Moses's face shone when he descended from the mountain where God had allowed him to see His glory, when God enters our lives, He works in us and makes our lives "brighter and more beautiful."

LIE: People are not trustworthy, and life will not work out.

TRUTH: God is trustworthy and will, in the end, work all things together for good.

> We know that in all things God works for the good of those who love him, who have been called according to his purpose.[4]

I CHOOSE TO DELIGHT IN GOD AND SIGNS OF HIS WORK IN THE WORLD AROUND ME.

We Have a Choice

EMOTION
HURT

THOUGHT
PEOPLE ARE NOT
TRUSTWORTHY, AND
LIFE WILL NOT
WORK OUT

BEHAVIOR
CRITICAL OF SELF
AND OTHERS

RELATIONSHIPS
SARCASTIC
AND COLD

CONSEQUENCE
CYNICAL

CONSEQUENCE
TRUSTING

RELATIONSHIPS
ENGAGED
AND CURIOUS

BEHAVIOR
BELIEVES IN THE
BEST IN OTHERS

THOUGHT
GOD IS TRUSTWORTHY
AND WILL, IN THE END,
WORK ALL THINGS OUT

I CHOOSE TO DELIGHT

EMOTION
HURT

THE BITTER TASTE OF CYNICISM

Now, if you are a true cynic, you aren't buying one word I am saying. And I get it because I am a recovering skilled cynic. In the months of my doubt, I picked up and practiced the skill of cynicism with precision. When healthy, I am a cheerleader, an eternal optimist, a passionate, hope-driven Enneagram 7. But the cynicism that took root in my heart in those months grew, masterfully hidden under the guise of coolness, fineness, and pride. In fact, I hardly could see the truth for what it was: I'd become angry, annoyed, and afraid.

A cynic is someone who "shows a disposition to disbelieve in the sincerity or goodness of human motives and actions."[5] And while this definition certainly played out for me, it hardly stopped there. Eventually I began to distrust God too.

For me, cynicism looked like a massive construction effort as I unknowingly built walls around my heart. I couldn't have told you at the time that I was evading true joy. If anything, my love of all things lighthearted tricked me into thinking I was plenty joyful.

Instead of my life becoming continually "brighter and more beautiful," as Paul described, my cynicism was like a dark cloud hovering over me. I was critical, distrusting, and distant.

Cynicism erodes our ability to see God rightly.

Cynicism at its root is a refusal to believe that God is in control and God is good. Cynicism is interpreting the world and God based on hurt you've experienced and the wounds that still lie gaping open. It forces you to look horizontally at people rather than vertically to God.

What I couldn't see then was that hurt was absolutely driving my behavior. I was so exhausted from everything—the oppression, the despair, the process of trying to find health—that I'd decided true joy probably just wasn't attainable. What I thought was joy was really just the delight of chronic distraction.

Then my growing cynicism and hurt were abruptly interrupted when I least expected it.

I've mentioned my friend Curt Thompson, who took some time recently to invest in some of us at a leadership retreat. During one of our many group chats, I projected a not-so-loving vibe. Or at least, that's what Curt later would say. My slightly raised eyebrows, my arms folded against my chest—everything about my posture communicated three words to Curt: *Leave. Me. Alone.*

Although I had experienced a lot of healing, I wasn't in the mood for invasive questions. I just wanted to eat queso with my friends and keep everyone else at what felt like a safe distance.

Periodically, after teasing out a bit of wisdom related to our minds, our hearts, our experiences making our way through life, Curt would check in by asking one person or another, "How are you feeling right now?"

I was fine as long as that question wasn't directed at me, so I played it cool, refusing to make eye contact. Partway through the first day, Curt dared to poke the bear. It was near the end of a group chat, and after allowing for a few moments of silence, Curt looked at me and asked, "How are you feeling right now?"

I stared at him for a second and then with a grin and a shrug said, "Good."

Who *was* I? This was a brilliant man whose work I esteem. We were lucky to have him there. And I was giving him the "Good" treatment? (I know it's grammatically correct to say, "Fine." But I say, "Good." It's going to be okay.)

Throughout the weekend my strategy worked pretty well, as the less I proved a willing participant, the less Curt seemed to call on me. But just when I thought I could escape our time together without divulging a stinking thing, something I never expected busted through my cynical guard.

Before I tell you what happened, I should mention that cynicism usually grows because we think we deserve better than we are getting. At the root of cynicism is crippling hurt. Cynicism says that nobody can be trusted, that we're never, ever safe.

My cynicism on our small retreat was prompted by an embarrassing thought. (Seriously, I can't believe I am about to tell you this.)

On the other side of my deep, dark spiritual spiral, I wasn't waking up at 3 a.m. anymore, but I was still a little bitter toward God. Here is why: I never would have said it out loud, but I had always lived with a delightful confidence that God liked me. That I was one of His favorites. I don't know whether God plays favorites, but I liked imagining His affection for me specifically.

The dark spiral of doubt left me carrying around the fear that He could just accidentally drop me into a crevice, like the bill you were supposed to pay that slipped into the gap between your desk and the wall. I felt as if I had fallen into a crack and He either hadn't noticed or hadn't cared enough to rescue me. I felt hurt by God.

My fear had given way to a protective shell of cynicism that blocked not only the potential for hurt but also the potential for joy.

Let's look back at Philippians 4, where Paul wrote,

> Rejoice in the Lord always; again I will say, rejoice. Let your
> reasonableness be known to everyone. The Lord is at hand; do
> not be anxious about anything, but in everything by prayer and
> supplication with thanksgiving let your requests be made known
> to God. And the peace of God, which surpasses all understanding,
> will guard your hearts and your minds in Christ Jesus.
>
> Finally, brothers, whatever is true, whatever is honorable,
> whatever is just, whatever is pure, whatever is lovely, whatever is
> commendable, if there is any excellence, if there is anything worthy

of praise, think about these things. What you have learned and
received and heard and seen in me—practice these things, and
the God of peace will be with you.[6]

Yes, I had been faithful to evict certain gloom-and-doom thoughts
from my mind, but unless I helped better thinking move in and settle
down, I'd keep trapping myself in terrible thoughts. There was something
here in Philippians 4 that I knew I should not miss. In my time with Curt,
I sensed Paul saying, "Look. Either you can try to guard your heart and
mind on your own, or you can surrender that guardianship to God."

My way of guarding my heart evidently involved sky-high walls and a
fondness for "Good" to mask my hurt and growing anger toward God and
others.

"How are you, Jennie?"

"Good! Doing great!"

"And now? Still good?"

"Better than good . . . really! You talk! Let's talk about you."

God's way was better. His way would lead me to peace.

Or that's how I read what Paul was saying, anyway. If I would practice
thinking what was honorable, what was just, what was lovely and excellent
and all the rest, I would experience the peace of God in my heart.

I really, really wanted that peace.

Then why was I still so cynical?

SURPRISED BY BEAUTY

The first time I ever saw a professional musical, I was a newlywed in my
early twenties. A Broadway company was touring, and *Les Misérables* had
come to our Little Rock stage. I'd been to school plays, and I remember
thinking, *How different can this be?*

Very different, it turned out.

Zac and I were just out of college and poor, but we scraped together enough funds for the cheapest tickets.

For the entirety of the show—as little Cosette, dreaming of a better life, sang "Castle on a Cloud," and as Éponine, who was desperately in love with Marius, who sadly was not desperately in love with her, sang "On My Own," and as the whole cast, it seemed, sang "One Day More"—I draped myself over the rail that separated me from the orchestra section down below, trying in vain to grasp all I was seeing: the rotating stage with its elaborate backdrops, the gorgeous costumes, the singing of phrases so beautiful they made me cry. I sat there stunned, as though I'd never seen a musical even once in my life, because as I realized that evening, until then I had not.

Beauty interrupts us, it awakens us, it undoes us, it cuts us open, and restarts our hearts. Beauty is God's evidence of something far more wonderful coming, a world beyond the one we can imagine, even in the most spectacular moments here. A God better than what we hope for. A God who blows our minds.

At this and a thousand other encounters with things that are excellent, that are lovely, that are true, we come away different from how we were before. We come away impacted. This, I think, is what Paul was hinting at when he told us what to set our thinking on.

Good things happen when we train our attention on that which is beautiful, on that which is authentic and compelling and good. What's more, beyond the obvious emotional experience, those good things from the hand of God can point us to the One who creates beauty, who is beautiful.

Cynicism puts our minds on things of this earth, and we lose hope. Beauty points our gaze toward the heavens and reminds us of hope.

Cynicism crumbles in the presence of beauty.

Pastor John Piper has told of his former professor Clyde Kilby's ten resolutions for mental health. Resolution six is this: "I shall open my eyes and ears. Once every day I shall simply stare at a tree, a flower, a cloud, or a person. I shall not then be concerned at all to ask what they are but simply be glad that they are."[7]

The first time I read those words, I thought back to my junior year of college, when I was leading a Bible study for twenty or so sophomores in my sorority. One night when we were scheduled to meet, I showed up having prepared a thorough lesson on one passage of Scripture. But once we all had settled in, I could tell that I was going to have to change tack. The girls sitting in the circle around me were in no shape to receive the message I'd prepared. They looked deflated and defeated, exasperated and exhausted and confused. Without saying a word, I ran outside the sorority house, pulled a leaf from a nearby tree, ran back inside, and sat down. "Girls," I said, "I want you to pass this leaf around the circle and really look at it. Look at the ridges, the lines, the veins. Look at the color. Look at the detail. Look at the shape, the contours, the stem."

It was a super cheesy object lesson, I'll admit, but you know what? That lesson stuck. God had gone to great lengths to craft this individual leaf; hadn't He applied even greater intention and care to our lives? We weren't alone. We weren't accidents. Our situations weren't hidden from God. Whatever it was that was weighing us down, God would gladly lift from our backs.

Think of *peacocks,* for crying out loud. The colors and detail, so unnecessarily delightful. Who but God would do that?

Or the way a symphony swells to something we can barely take in. My countenance and posture lift when I hear it.

Or the video of the man playing his upright piano in his living room while surrounded by two feet of standing water left in Hurricane Harvey's wake.[8]

Or the patterns of a flower's petals—three for lilies, five for buttercups, twenty-one for chicory, thirty-four for daisies. That doesn't just *happen,* you know? God thought of them and whipped them out.

I CHOOSE DELIGHT

Or the perfect spirals both of hurricanes and of seashells. Or the structured flight patterns of birds. Or the design of our elbows and fingers and toes. It's everywhere if you look, if you only have eyes to see.

There is such intention.
Such craftsmanship.
Such incredible functionality.
Such beauty.
Such *proof.*

Scientists wonder whether it's all mere coincidence. I know better. You likely do too. "The heavens declare the glory of God, and the sky above proclaims his handwork," the psalmist declared.[9] **Goodness is meant not to merely make us feel good but to point us to God.**

That day at the leadership retreat, God busted through my crossed arms and "I'm good" scowl. And of all things, God used an essay. A simple, beautiful essay about the chaos of unexpected difficulties. While the story line of "Welcome to Holland" centers on finding out your child has special needs, the truths tucked inside apply to so many situations.

My friend Mica quoted it from memory, and it penetrated my carefully constructed walls of protection.

The story[10] tells of planning a wonderful trip to Italy, buying the travel books and making the itinerary. But then you get off the plane and realize you've landed in Holland. Holland isn't bad, but your friends are all having the Italian vacation you dreamed of, and you are here in Holland with no one and no plan.

And I wept because I had been in Holland alone and wanted to know why God seemed okay with it. Why would He abandon me to plans I didn't create and didn't want without consulting me? Why had He let me slip into the dark crack beside the desk and left me there?

Saying it out loud showed me the hurt I didn't even know I was feeling—and eased my pain.

Those things Paul said to think about—all things beautiful and excellent and just—they are what soften a doubting heart, what bring sanity to a chaotic mind map.

An entire weekend with some of my favorite people and a gifted counselor, all to draw us out, and God used an *essay* to unlock my tightly crossed arms.

Beauty is evidence of something beyond ourselves. Beauty is evidence of a world yet to come.

Beauty is evidence of a Creator who is loving and profoundly delightful.

Beauty floods in and interrupts when, instead of cynicism, we choose trust.

Breaking Down Our Walls

Michiel van Elk, a researcher at the University of Amsterdam, recently explained how he is using MRIs of the brain to show that feelings of awe shut down selfishness. When we are in awe of something, we become less self-centered, more others-centered, and more connected to others around us.[11]

We worship when we experience awe.

And cynicism and worship cannot coexist.

I think about how cynical I'd become, about how my arms-folded self just *wasn't* going to choose to trust. I didn't *want* someone coming for me—which is, of course, the problem. Cynicism is especially powerful as a tool in Satan's hands because when you and I are struck by it, we don't see our need to be helped.

We think we're just fine, thank you very much.

The truth? We desperately need Jesus.

Bruno Mars released a love song years ago that says, "I'd catch a grenade for ya . . . jump in front of a train for ya."[12] While it was a catchy tune, I don't think Bruno would really do that for ya, you know?

But guess who would?

Guess who did?

Jesus, Son of God. He faced the greatest sacrifice to bust through our cool "I don't need anybody" attitude, our intellect and shame and doubt. He entered our reality and arrested us with the story we longed to be true.

A few months ago, while I was speaking at an event hours away, a bit of a crisis was unfolding back at home. My younger daughter, Caroline, had accidentally locked herself in the upstairs bathroom and couldn't get out. Our house in Dallas is approximately a hundred years old, which means that the window frames have about eighteen coats of paint, the floors are not perfectly level, and the door handles are prone to just falling off. Which is what had happened on one side of the door for sweet Caroline, leaving her trapped in the bathroom.

Zac was with me at the event, frantically responding to text messages, first from Caroline and then from our son Conner, who was living a few miles away at college but had providentially happened to stop by the house to pick up a few things. It would be two hours after the exchange that I'd learn all that had gone down, and I laughed until I cried.

Zac to all Allen kids but Caroline:	Hey, you guys go rescue Caro who is locked in bathroom.
Zac to Caroline:	Caroline, are you out?
Conner to Zac:	This is bad
Zac to Conner:	Mom is onstage
Conner to Zac:	Can I break the door
Conner, a few seconds later, to Zac:	There is no other solution right now and I gotta go to school
Conner, now on a mission, to Zac:	Nothing else is working
Conner to Zac:	[Sends a selfie, with him now wearing his high school football helmet and full pads and jersey.]
Conner to Zac:	Door is going down
Zac to Conner:	No
Conner to Zac:	I got my pads on dad can I just get her out this is not working
Zac to Conner:	No
Kate to Zac and Conner:	I'm coming home in a sec
Zac to all kids:	Caroline just wait till mom is finished and I will call you
Zac to Caroline:	In the meantime just do what you always do in the bathroom. That ought to keep you busy for a couple of hours.

In the selfie, Conner's expression is one of outright determination, of commitment and concern, of "Caroline, I'm comin' for you!"

And, friend, this is what I picture when I think of you out there fighting all kinds of darkness, spiraling out . . .

Jesus came for us—for you and me, with our arms crossed. Bitter, cranky, unsure, doubting, cynical, negative us.

I know I said the interrupting thought that shifts all the others is *I have a choice.*

And there is one reason that is true. It's because Jesus first chose us.

It's because He busted down the door and rescued us in His beauty and kindness. He suited up and came for us. And that is why we aren't cynical, expecting the worst.

Because we have been promised a forever better than we can imagine.

Why don't they ever listen to me?

But I was right!

You don't care about me.

I will prove them wrong.

None of this is my fault.

Doesn't anyone care about my needs?

I've got this.

Less Important

I Choose to Serve God and Others

NOT LONG AGO, I SNAPPED AT ONE OF MY IF:GATHERING colleagues. Worse still, this was a new coworker, someone who doesn't yet know me and thus doesn't know that I'm generally not a snappy person. Worst of all, I didn't apologize. At least, not at first.

I won't go into detail about what she did that catalyzed my—let's say "passionate"—response. But I reacted with such agitation, such animation, such temper, that I completely shut her down. I saw that I'd shut her down. Only an imbecile wouldn't have noticed that. But did I remedy the situation by asking for forgiveness? Nope. I went on with my day. (Just a little aside: If you want to intern at IF:Gathering, please don't let this incident discourage you from applying. Ninety-nine percent of the time, I am really, really nice.)

Later that afternoon, after I left the office, I thought about calling this new team member to apologize, but then my train of thought embarked on a journey of self-justification: *Maybe it was no big deal to her. She's probably already moved on. Maybe by calling and drawing attention to my little oops, I'll only be stirring things up.*

I thought about how I'd been justified in my reaction because her perspective had been so far off base. I also thought about how tired I was and how hungry I was and how I deserved a little grace. Yes, I felt sure that if she knew all the stress I was under, she'd want to give me grace.

So I gave myself grace.

Had I been paying closer attention, I would have recognized the lie that my self-esteem is a valid guide for navigating life.

Maybe you can relate? We compare and contrast, justify and judge, and spend a ridiculous amount of time contemplating our identity and place in this world. Maybe this is why the apostle Paul cautioned us not to think of ourselves more highly than we ought. Instead, we're to "honor one another above [ourselves]."[1]

But developing such an approach to life requires us to deliberately and repeatedly interrupt the natural trajectory of our thoughts.

One of my favorite thinkers on the Christ-following life is the nineteenth-century pastor and prolific writer Andrew Murray. One of his best-known books is on this subject of humility. In fact, that's the title of the book: *Humility.* Not very creative, but sometimes plain works best.

In his book Murray wrote at length about the nuances of considering others "more significant than yourselves," referring to such humility in lofty terms like "participation in the life of Jesus" and "the place of entire dependence on God" and "the only soil in which the graces root" and "the disposition which prepares the soul for living on trust" and "our redemption" and "our saviour."[2]

He also said this: "The question is often asked, how we can count others better than ourselves, when we see that they are far below us in wisdom and in holiness, in natural gifts, or in grace received."[3]

Now, see—this is why I love Andrew Murray. He knew exactly how our minds work against us, and he had the courage to put our true thoughts into words!

Pride says,

He's the one who's wrong.

Her overreaction is what caused this mess.

I am not that bad.

My thought about snapping at my colleague was, *It wasn't that big of a deal.*

You probably know where this story is going.

For the next twenty-four hours, a passage from Scripture kept coming to mind. Whenever my mouth gets me into trouble, in fact, I tend to think of this passage in 1 Peter 2. The context is all about how we should live as God's chosen, special people, and the short answer is that we're to follow the example of Jesus. But I'm guessing you knew that!

Here's where it gets complicated, at least for me. Jesus, who came to earth from heaven and took up the form of a human body, lived His life flawlessly and was declared by God to be sinless in the end. This includes the tense confrontation with the religious leaders who decided He would be killed on a Roman cross. This, for a man who, according to verse 22, "committed no sin, neither was deceit found in his mouth."

So Jesus found Himself standing before powerful men, men who held in their hands the power to send Him to His death. They were questioning Him—reviling Him, the text says—asking Him to plead His case. Jesus faced a key decision: How would He respond?

The answer convicts me every time. "When he was reviled," verse 23 says, "he did not revile in return; when he suffered, he did not threaten, but continued entrusting himself to him who judges justly."

Ugh.

Jesus did nothing wrong and held His tongue when falsely accused; my teammate sorta, kinda, maybe misspoke, and I lashed out in response?

THE WAY OF HUMILITY

We've been talking for several chapters now about various choices we can make when confronted with toxic thought patterns, about *different thoughts* we can choose to think, thoughts that reflect the mind of Christ.

When we're tempted, for example, to use busyness to distract ourselves from dealing with the truth, we can choose instead to be still in the presence of God.

When our minds are consumed with anxiety and doubts and fears, we can choose instead to remember what's true about God.

We can think about His nearness.

We can think about His goodness.

We can think about His provision.

We can think about His love.

When we're tempted to believe we're all alone in this world, we can choose instead the thought, *The Spirit of God lives inside of me, and because of that, I'm never alone. There are people who love me, who want to be with me. I can reach out to them instead of sitting here, stuck.*

When we're tempted to think cynical thoughts—that life is worthless, that our efforts are pointless, that nothing matters in the end, that no one can be trusted—we can choose instead to open ourselves up to the world around us, taking delight in God Himself and all He has done for us.

These are all choices that we can make to reconfigure our thinking patterns and help ourselves become whom we long to be.

This brings us to our fifth weapon for shifting out of harmful patterns of thinking: *humility.* One of the enemies of our minds especially rampant in this generation is the inflated view of self being handed to us all over social media, in the shows and movies we watch, even in the self-help books we read. We're fed a continuous message of how much we matter, how very important we are—and we believe every word of the deceiver.

We can make a different choice.

When the enemy invites us to taste the fruit of self-importance and "be like God,"[4] we can choose instead to take up our cross and follow Jesus, knowing that our identity is anchored in Him alone.

But everything in our human nature will fight against it.

LIE: The more self-esteem I have, the better life will go for me.

TRUTH: The more I choose God and others over myself, the more joyful I will be.

> In your relationships with one another, have the same mindset as Christ Jesus:
>
> Who, being in very nature God,
>   did not consider equality with God something
>   to be used to his own advantage;
> rather, he made himself nothing
>   by taking the very nature of a servant,
>   being made in human likeness.
> And being found in appearance as a man,
>   he humbled himself
>   by becoming obedient to death—even death
>   on a cross![5]

I CHOOSE TO SERVE GOD AND OTHERS OVER SERVING MYSELF.

I Have a Choice

EMOTION
ANGER

THOUGHT
I AM BETTER THAN
OTHER PEOPLE

BEHAVIOR
SELF-PROMOTER AND
SELF-PROTECTOR

RELATIONSHIPS
DRAINED AND
NEGLECTED

CONSEQUENCE
UNKNOWN AND
FEELING UNLOVED

CONSEQUENCE
SELFLESSLY
SERVES OTHERS

RELATIONSHIPS
GENEROUS
AND JOYFUL

BEHAVIOR
PROMOTES AND
PROTECTS OTHERS

THOUGHT
THE MORE I CHOOSE
GOD AND OTHERS OVER
MYSELF, THE MORE
JOYFUL I WILL BE

I CHOOSE TO
SERVE GOD AND OTHERS

EMOTION
ANGER

I recently posted on Instagram this quote often attributed to Andrew Murray:

> Humility is perfect quietness of heart. . . . It is to expect nothing, to wonder at nothing that is done to me, to feel nothing done against me. It is to be at rest when nobody praises me and when I am blamed or despised. It is to have a blessed home in the Lord, where I can go in and shut the door, and kneel to my Father in secret, and am at peace, as in a deep sea of calmness, when all around and above is trouble.

The comments in response to that post were priceless:
"Wow. This is difficult."
"How rare."
"Whoa. That hurts."

Humility is impossibly opposite of the ways of this world. Our spinning thoughts can hardly comprehend being at rest instead of jockeying for approval.

Yet, interestingly enough, **we weren't built to be the center of our own worlds.**

Self-importance can mess with those beautiful mirror neurons I told you about a few chapters ago. Do you remember what they do? They help us empathize with others and connect on a visceral level. When we are puffed up with thoughts of how important we are, our mirror neurons are impaired. That's why, in my spiraling of self-importance, truly understanding my coworker's point of view was nearly impossible.[6]

SOMETHING LESS THAN GREAT

The apostle Paul embodied the idea of being at rest even when being blamed or despised. While imprisoned—most likely in a house-arrest situation—wondering whether he would be executed, he declared his central desire to rejoice, to praise God, to spread the good news wherever he was. "Whatever gain I had, I counted as loss for the sake of Christ," he said.

> Indeed, I count everything as loss because of the surpassing worth of knowing Christ Jesus my Lord. For his sake I have suffered the loss of all things and count them as rubbish, in order that I may gain Christ and be found in him, not having a righteousness of my own that comes from the law, but that which comes through faith in Christ, the righteousness from God that depends on faith—that I may know him and the power of his resurrection, and may share his sufferings, becoming like him in his death, that by any means possible I may attain the resurrection from the dead.[7]

Paul possessed an incredible disregard for his losses and accomplishments alike. He disregarded the things that the rest of the world esteems. I mean, he even disregarded himself. He couldn't care less what happened to him, just as long as he could know Jesus better. In fact, those things the rest of us count as important? "Rubbish!" Paul said of them.

I find these insights from Paul staggering, especially in our day and age. If I had to name the most destructive line of thinking in our twenty-first-century culture, it's our incessant quest to be great. We spend a lot of effort trying to become distinct, successful, smarter, stronger, thinner . . . great. We love being great. It's so great to be so great.

We want to be great—as in, *accomplished and successful.* Sure, we may couch it in acceptable terms, like "doing great things for the kingdom" or "making God's name famous." But somehow our thoughts subtly become centered not on Him but on ourselves—how we can achieve our goals, realize our dreams, enlarge our influence, position ourselves for success.

Let me tell you a quick story. For as long as I have known her, my friend Heather has been busting at the seams to use her gifts of writing and teaching. But for whatever reason, she won't go for it! Despite many of us encouraging her because she is truly gifted to do this.

Recently we were on the phone catching up, and she expressed some critical perspectives about other people who are running their races.

These are people we both love, people who are building and serving and risking their guts out.

Now, why would my perfectly lovely, godly, creative friend be so critical? Because—kind of like (she is going to hate this) the grumpy middle-aged men eating nachos in the stands while deciding how the Cowboys should have called that game to beat the Chiefs—she was in the stands, eating nachos, with no skin in the game.

We spend a lot of time looking around at others—not so we can encourage them in their growth but so we can figure out how we measure up. We convince ourselves that God wants us to be amazing. We are all about empowerment. **But lasting joy will come only when God is in the center; not when I am empowered but when I rest in His power.**

When our thoughts are consumed with ourselves, we forget how very much we need Jesus. We buy the lie of self-empowerment: "You've got this." We forget that we are called to take up our cross and follow Him, to share in His sufferings, and "to live a life worthy of the calling you have received. Be completely humble and gentle; be patient, bearing with one another in love. Make every effort to keep the unity of the Spirit through the bond of peace."[8]

I react unfairly to a coworker, and then I feel angsty and guilty and mad. To make myself feel better, I stuff those feelings and just move on. Later I feel guilty again, but instead of apologizing, I start listing the reasons I was right and she was wrong.

Notice any trends in the litany below?

I feel angsty.

I feel guilty.

I feel mad.

I stuff those emotions.

I move on.

I list reasons.

I decide I am right.

I, I, I, I, I.

A puffed-up pride fills my senses and causes me to keep justifying, defending, abdicating responsibility, and refusing to budge.

I am the centerpiece in this little scenario, the one that has fractured the tie between my coworker and me.

Humility. It just feels so *difficult* sometimes, you know? I am no better than a toddler who would rather lose all his favorite things than say, "I'm sorry. I was wrong."

Then I remember Jesus.

Guiltless and wrongfully accused.

Yet still completely humble of heart.

Our friend the apostle Paul pointed to Jesus as our guide for how to let go of greatness. In Philippians 2, he wrote, "In your relationships with one another, have the same mindset as Christ Jesus."[9]

I CHOOSE HUMILITY

And what was that mind-set?

> Though he was in the form of God, [he] did not count equality
> with God a thing to be grasped, but emptied himself, by taking
> the form of a servant, being born in the likeness of men. And being
> found in human form, he humbled himself by becoming obedient
> to the point of death, even death on a cross.[10]

He emptied Himself by taking the form of a servant.

He humbled Himself by becoming obedient to death.

Does this sound as convicting to you as it does to me?

A sacrifice requiring emptiness, ultimate meekness, devastating lowliness of heart—this wasn't merely a kind act from Jesus for humankind. It was also intended to be an example—as in, a move that *His followers would consistently make.*

Inviting the death of self-centeredness.

Enduring the death of dreams.

Allowing for the death of hyperconsumerism.

Being *least awesome, least liked, last.*

Jesus humbled Himself deeply so that we'd be compelled to live lives of deep humility too.

That is, if we so *choose.*

THE UPSIDE OF HUMILITY

When we realize we've bought into the lie of our own greatness and we make the shift to choose humility, we then can follow the example of Jesus, who "did not count equality with God a thing to be grasped . . ."

who "emptied himself . . ."

who took on "the form of a servant . . ."

who "humbled himself . . ."

who became "obedient to the point of death, even death on a cross."

When we mimic the qualities that motivated these acts, we put God in His rightful place. We replace the lie of our greatness with the truth of who God is—and how needy we are apart from Him. Humility becomes the only logical posture of our hearts.

The day after my little lashing-out episode and under undeniable conviction from God, I pulled aside my coworker and asked for her forgiveness. "I need to apologize for something I said yesterday," I started. "I was wrong, and I'm so sorry. My reaction was really unfair."

You know how I wondered whether maybe she hadn't even noticed the slight, whether maybe she'd looked past it and just moved on? Yeah. Not so much.

"Can I cool off for a while," she asked quietly, "and then we can sit down and talk this out?"

I had hurt her—deeply. She'd been miserable for twenty-four hours.

The Bible makes it clear that humility comes with benefits,[11] but let me provide three specific benefits here, keeping that unfortunate situation with my coworker in mind.

Humility Helps Us Let Go of Being Awesome

I know something about myself that I used to spend a lot of time trying to cover up: get too close to me and I will disappoint you quickly and often.

And while I hate that it is true, it is true. Pedestals make miserable homes, and the sooner my new coworker realizes that she's working for a sinner who happens to be leading an organization (and who happens to maybe snap at her one time and then feel terrible about it later—ahem), the better.

Now, I am not justifying my behavior, but the truth is, I'm going to make mistakes. I'm going to be selfish and sometimes unthoughtful and short. I'm going to let her down. I'm not going to *want* to do these things, but now and again they will happen. I'm absolutely going to screw up. How do I know these things?

Because I've come to understand that I'm just not all that great.

Before you rush to my defense: *I think this understanding is the goal.* Caring little about what you think about me. Caring little about what even I think about me. Do you know how much freedom we could experience, if we prized these two simple truths?

My son Cooper is ten years old and is the walking, talking epitome of self-importance. I adore that kid, but I stand by my assessment. I think we're all that way at ten years old: we're big deals—at least, we think we are. (Middle school usually takes care of such things, so I'm going to let it ride.)

Anyway, Cooper, who cares more about clothes and shoes than his two teenage sisters combined, came downstairs the other morning wearing the fancy Air Jordan shoes that his grandmother bought him and reminded me that he "needs" a leather jacket. He's been asking for one for weeks. I don't know which of his basketball heroes he saw clad in a leather jacket, but now Cooper's life will not be complete until he has one of his own.

"I just want to be *awesome*," his pleading eyes say to me.

And are you and I any different? At ten years old and at forty, our eyes say the very same thing.

When I (finally) chose to humble myself with that coworker and ask her to forgive me for what I had done, I was relieved. I had done the backward thing God asks of us, that thing you and I tend to hate.

I'd humbled myself.

I'd apologized.

I'd made things right again.

Just today, she and I were texting about our tiff, able to laugh about it now.

I know that it's all the rage these days to talk about how amazing everyone is, how we're each *special* and *talented* and *enough*. But I have to tell you, I don't find these ideas in Scripture. We find our "enoughness" only in Christ. If anything, God's Word tells us to camp out on the opposite view from the one our culture holds: when we're weak, it's actually a good thing, because Christ's power is made more evident in us.[12]

I happen to think that this is *fantastic* news.

I recently read an article about the problems that come with success. It included this quote from a man who, by earthly standards, has achieved awesomeness. "Imagine life as two barometers," he said.

> One is how the world sees you. The other is how you feel
> about yourself. As your worldly position rises, your self-
> image crashes. People abuse themselves with fine food
> or drink or drugs or sex—so they can avoid getting too
> successful. Why do CEOs who are sitting on top of the
> world have a problem with self-esteem? It's simple: People
> who feel like bags of [. . .] overcompensate and act like gods
> of creation.[13]

Self-importance always self-implodes. Because we weren't built to live like gods.

Yet with all the evidence against it, achievement is still the most popular drug of our generation.

Listen. There is a reason we don't like to hang out in nursing homes and hospitals. There's a reason we posture. There's a reason we buy stuff labeled "anti-aging." There's a reason we drive more car than we can afford. There's a reason we notice labels.

We all want to be awesome, even as Christ is the only awesome one.

This is one of the most freeing and rarely embraced truths of following Christ: Because of the sacrifice of Jesus, we get His awesomeness as part of the deal. We get His righteousness. We get forgiveness. We get rest. We get grace for our souls.

Humility reminds us of this truth. It says, "Relax. Your only hope is Jesus."

It is good news and grants us the exhale we all are craving.

Humility Helps Us See People as God Sees Them

Earlier I told you that one of the reasons I love Andrew Murray is that he had the courage to admit what you and I probably think from time to time, which is something along the lines of *How am I supposed to be humble with* them *(whoever they are), when they're so hurtful/annoying/wrong?*

Here's the rest of his thinking on that: "The question proves at once how little we understand what real lowliness of mind is. True humility comes when, in the light of God, we have seen ourselves to be nothing, have consented to part with and cast away self, to let God be all."[14]

To "cast away self." We don't use that phrase anymore, but it's a good one. It means to put our own concerns and considerations aside, to put them far from us, to put them on God. Matthew 6:33 promises as we cast away our own worries, God promises to care for us. An amazing thing happens when we "cast away self," which is that we then have space to consider *others*. When we're not busy being consumed with our own selves, we notice other people in the world, people we might be able to serve. We see them with fresh perspective. We see their fragility and their need.

When I woke up to the fact that I needed to apologize to that co-worker, my empathy woke up too. In going to my teammate and acknowledging my misstep and saying "Will you please forgive me?" I was able to see things from her perspective. I was able to absorb how damaging and wrong my actions had been.

The fiery Baptist preacher Charles Spurgeon once said, "Your own spiritual beauty may be very much measured by what you can see in other people."[15] It was only after I'd chosen to humble myself that I could see this coworker's frustration, her angst, her pain.

"Get wisdom, and whatever you get, get insight," Proverbs 4:7 says. Humility gets both to us *fast*.

Humility Helps Us Treat People as Jesus Would

There's a third benefit to choosing humility, which is that we can show up for those in need. You'll recall that, in response to my apology, my colleague asked for some time to cool down. Apart from a posture of humility, who would indulge such a request? *You need time to think about whether you'll accept my apology?*

At her request, I remember thinking, *No. I want to make this better now!* But guess what? It wasn't about me. She had every right to make that request.

Humility says, "Not only do I see you, but I choose to elevate your needs above mine."

So I said—and eventually meant—"Of course, friend. Take as much time as you need. I'll be here when you're ready to talk."

An Unlikely Pleasure

Not long ago, my daughter Kate and I were talking about a show we liked on Netflix, when she said, "I love it. But I also hate it, you know?" She went on to say that she's been realizing that the completely socially acceptable choice to veg out with Netflix is hardly a benign one. "When I spend a night doing that," Kate said, "instead of, say, reading my Bible or sitting with God in prayer, I get pointed in a totally different direction than if I'd done the more life-giving thing."

She laughed. "I don't know if that makes me a nerd or what."

"We should all be so nerdy," I said.

Here's the thing. I believe the Bible. I want to live what it says. I want to be more like Jesus each day. And despite these noble intentions, the fact is, I can't conjure humility myself. There is a reason our first choice in this part of the book involved being still and seeking God. We can't become more like Him apart from Him imparting Himself to us. Humility comes only when I choose to be with Him and depend on Him instead of buying the lie that I am enough.

A favorite Bible dictionary of mine defines *humility* this way: "A condition of lowliness or affliction in which one experiences a loss of power and prestige."

It then clarifies the definition with this: "Outside of biblical faith, humility in this sense would not usually be considered a virtue. Within the context of the Judeo-Christian tradition, however, humility is considered the proper attitude of human beings toward their Creator. Humility is a grateful and spontaneous awareness that life is a gift, and it is manifested as an ungrudging and unhypocritical acknowledgment of absolute dependence upon God."[16]

Outside of biblical faith, humility would be *lunacy*. Who wants *less* power, *less* prestige? But within biblical faith, it is virtuous, this utter dependence on God.

If God created me and loves me, why would I want to steal any of His glory? I can't steal His glory because I am just human—but why would I even try?

The truth is, our hearts aren't really after power; they're after joy. And the deception we buy into is that somehow joy will come when we have power. **Joy comes when we lay aside our power and rest in God's.** Joy comes when we put the emphasis where it belongs: on God's awesomeness, not our own.[17]

There is grace for the process. Cooper is learning this truth, right along with you and me.

My not-so-little guy is growing by the minute and needed new shoes, so tonight we headed to our sporting goods store as a family. He'd earned some money and could afford the shoes all his friends wanted. But he chose some that were simple and cost much less. He was excited about them.

As Zac tucked him in tonight, out of the blue Cooper said, "Dad, I didn't want to get the shoes all the cool kids have. I feel like Jesus wouldn't want me to wear shoes that say 'Look at me.' I can still be cool with these. Not super cool, but cool enough."

Oh, that you and I would align our thoughts not so our lives would say "Look at me" but so everything about us would declare "Look at You, Jesus!"

My prayer for myself—and also for you—is that we'd be utterly dependent on God. That we'd seek Him and find Him and learn from Him and lean into Him, that we'd be in this world as Jesus Himself was. That we'd accept every invitation into humility, prizing others' needs above our own. That we wouldn't despise that which will grow us up by reminding us to bow lower, and lower still.

"Every Christian virtually passes through these two stages in his pursuit of humility," said our good friend Andrew Murray.

> In the first he fears and flees and seeks deliverance from all that can humble him. . . . He prays for humility, at times very earnestly; but in his secret heart he prays more, if not in word, then in wish, to be kept from the very things that will make him humble. . . . It has not yet become his joy and only pleasure. He cannot yet say, "Most gladly do I glory in weakness, I take pleasure in whatever humbles me."

But can we hope to reach the stage in which this will be the case? Undoubtedly. And what will it be that brings us there? *That which brought Paul there—a new revelation of the Lord Jesus.*[18]

To "take pleasure in whatever humbles me." Man. Such a lofty goal. Such a freed-up way of thinking about our circumstances and the people around us.

"Father, help me choose the pleasure of humility today." It's a place to start.

It's not fair.

I will always feel like this.

At this point, I'm just trying to survive.

I'll never fully recover from
everything that's happened to me.

I'll never be happy again.

I don't deserve this.

My life wasn't supposed to be like this.

I want to move on, but I can't.

You wouldn't believe what I've been through.

Why don't I get the good breaks?

Not Overcome

I Choose to Be Grateful

MY GOOD FRIEND BROOKE WAS DISILLUSIONED AND frustrated. She had a college degree and believed there had to be something that suited her skills better than a job on her feet all day, working retail. Yet six days a week, she made the twenty-minute drive from her apartment to the Anthropologie store where she worked, fuming all the while about how far her life was from what she had envisioned for herself.

Then she heard something that opened her eyes to the real problem with her life.

"I remember the day I started listening to Scripture in my car," she told me. Barely two minutes into the audio stream, a passage caught her off guard.

The text being read was Philippians 1: "I thank my God in all my remembrance of you," Paul said, "always in every prayer of mine for you all making my prayer with joy, because of your partnership in the gospel from the first day until now. And I am sure of this, that he who began a good work in you will bring it to completion at the day of Jesus Christ."[1]

Paul was thankful—so thankful. He was thankful for his fellow believers, thankful for the diligence of his coworkers, thankful for where he was stationed even though he was under house arrest. The man was minding his mind.

As Brooke drove to work and listened to these words from Philippians, she couldn't help but be struck by the contrast between Paul and her.

Paul had been imprisoned for preaching the gospel, yet despite this unjust treatment, he saw fit to give thanks. He saw fit to keep praying, to keep ministering, to keep striving alongside fellow believers for the hearts of women and men.

What had she seen fit to do? According to her: *complain*.

But her thinking shifted that day. "Jennie," she said to me, "I saw my life in a new way." She realized she could choose how she viewed her work. As she entered the store that morning, she saw her coworkers with fresh eyes. She decided to forge real relationships with them, watching for ways to care for and serve them. She began interacting differently with customers, seeing them not as nameless strangers but as real people with real stories who might need real grace. She began using her drive time to pray. A month into these new practices, she told me that she no longer despised her job. In fact, she *loved* it.

Instead of fixating on the unfairness of her circumstance and stewing over how she deserved something better, something that used her skills and education to best effect, she began to see her less-than-fulfilling job as an opportunity to advance the kingdom.

God had set her in a strategic place to love others, and now she was excited to be part of His plan.

Instead of looking for things to complain about, my friend was now looking for reasons to give thanks. She didn't know it at the time, but she was doing herself far greater favors than merely ensuring a more pleasant drive to and from work and deeper satisfaction through her workday. She was *rewiring her brain* by choosing gratitude. She was allowing God to remake her, body and mind.

Your Brain on Gratitude

Victimhood is yet another enemy of our minds that keeps us fixated on something other than the God of the universe, believing the lie that we are at the mercy of circumstances.

But we have a choice. We can center our thoughts on the certainty that, **no matter what comes, we are upheld securely by God's righteous right hand.**[2]

And that will shift our minds toward gratitude.

A few years ago, the magazine *Psychology Today* referenced a study from the National Institutes of Health that reported that subjects who "showed more gratitude overall had higher levels of activity in the hypothalamus," which, I will tell you, in case you, too, were doodling during your college biology lecture, is the part of your brain that controls bodily functions—eating, drinking, sleeping, the whole works.[3]

Doing something as straightforward as saying "Thank you" is like a tune-up for your inner world.

Expressing gratitude caused subjects to experience an increase in dopamine hits, the reward neurotransmitter that makes the brain happy. In short, each time a subject expressed gratitude, the brain said, "Ooh! Do it again!" In this way, feeling gratitude led to feeling more gratitude, which led to feeling more and more gratitude still. "Once you start seeing things to be grateful for, your brain starts looking for more things to be grateful for."[4]

Research has revealed seven key benefits to those who make gratitude a practice:

1. "Gratitude opens the door to more relationships." Something as simple as saying "Thanks" to someone you know only slightly makes that person more likely to look for friendship with you.

2. "Gratitude improves physical health." When people are thankful, they exercise more, make better decisions about their health, and experience fewer aches and pains.

3. "Gratitude improves psychological health." It reduces harmful emotions such as jealousy, frustration, and regret.

4. "Gratitude enhances empathy and reduces aggression." One study found that "grateful people are more likely to behave in a prosocial manner," which I think is a nice way of saying a grateful person is less likely to be a jerk.

5. "Grateful people sleep better," which is a good enough reason in itself for you and me to be grateful.

6. "Gratitude improves self-esteem" and allows a person to genuinely celebrate the achievements of others instead of wishing she'd been the one to achieve.

7. "Gratitude increases mental strength," helping a person lower stress, overcome trauma, and increase resilience, even during bad times.[5]

Just one question: If gratitude is this good for us—and it is; God designed us that way—then why is it so hard to be grateful when life isn't going the way we think it should?

ARE YOU READY FOR A SHIFT?

Ever wonder why some people seem happier than you, even if they are going through more difficult circumstances? Maybe you have visited Christians in developing countries, thinking you were there to minister to them in their need, only to realize through their smiles and joy and selflessness that you were the one who had the need.

Yeah, me too.

When Paul wrote his letter to the Philippians, the greatest exposition on joy ever written, he was actually bound in chains under house arrest. Paul apprehended something we in our cocoon of comfort in the West rarely realize. He understood that because we have been made new creations, we have the Spirit's power and a choice to make. Changing our minds *is* possible.

We do not have to spin—because we know our happiness is anchored in something greater than anything we can see here and now.

So this prompts a second question: What are you looking toward to make you happy? Whether it is opioids or people's praise, whatever causes you to experience strong emotions of either happiness or disappointment—that is likely the thing you are living for. And it is very likely ruining your life.

If all Paul saw were his circumstances and his inability to end his imprisonment, he would surely have been despondent. But his circumstances didn't dictate his thoughts. It was his love of Jesus and trust in a good, loving, in-control God that consumed his mind and gave him purpose. And the same power that raised Christ from the dead, the same Spirit that empowered Paul to trust in the direst circumstances, is fully accessible to you and me. Right now.

As we make the shift from debilitating lines of thinking to thoughts that are helpful and God honoring and wise, we can make the choice to be *grateful*. We can be people who consistently and sincerely give thanks, regardless of our wounded pasts or the circumstances we now face.

LIE: I am a victim to my circumstances.

TRUTH: My circumstances provide opportunities to experience the goodness of God.

Rejoice always, pray without ceasing, give thanks in all circumstances; for this is the will of God in Christ Jesus for you.[6]

I CHOOSE TO BE GRATEFUL NO MATTER WHAT LIFE BRINGS.

Paul certainly made this choice, as evidenced by the fact that he was quick to express gratitude for the believers at Philippi despite the mind-boggling pain he'd endured. If anyone knew suffering, it was Paul. In Acts 9:15–16 God told Ananias, "Go, for he [Paul, also known as Saul] is a chosen instrument of mine to carry my name before the Gentiles and kings and the children of Israel. For I will show him how much he must suffer for the sake of my name."

And suffer Paul certainly did.

In the book of Acts, we read that Paul experienced

- having his life threatened in Damascus
- having his life threatened in Jerusalem
- being run out of Antioch
- possible stoning at Iconium
- stoning and being left for dead in Lystra
- opposition and controversy
- the loss of Barnabas, his friend and colaborer in the gospel
- being beaten with rods and imprisoned
- being cast out of Philippi
- having his life threatened in Thessalonica
- being forced out of Berea
- being mocked in Athens
- being apprehended by a mob in Jerusalem

I Have a Choice

EMOTION
SELF-PITY

CONSEQUENCE
JOYFUL

THOUGHT
I AM A VICTIM TO
MY CIRCUMSTANCES

RELATIONSHIPS
FORGIVING

BEHAVIOR
COMPLAINS

BEHAVIOR
GIVES THANKS

RELATIONSHIPS
PLACES BLAME

THOUGHT
MY CIRCUMSTANCES
ARE AN OPPORTUNITY
TO EXPERIENCE GOD

I CHOOSE TO BE GRATEFUL

CONSEQUENCE
CONSISTENTLY
UNHAPPY

EMOTION
SELF-PITY

- being arrested and detained by the Romans
- being flogged/scourged
- being imprisoned for more than two years in Caesarea
- being shipwrecked on the island of Malta
- a snakebite
- being imprisoned in Rome[7]

Recorded elsewhere, Paul endured confrontation, the betrayal of friends, more accusations, whippings, beatings, stoning, imprisonments, robberies, and again, being left for dead.[8] Had any *one* of these things happened in the course of my lifetime, I'd center my whole world on the event. I'd give interviews about it. I'd write a book about it. I'd craft talks about it. I'd tell *everyone* how bad it had been. I'd cast myself as the victim, something Paul never chose to do. In what has been dubbed our "victimhood culture," Paul certainly would have stood out.

And what are we complaining about? Anything and everything, it seems.

I'm telling you, there's a far better way—the way of gratitude.

God made sure to include a clear call to thankfulness in Scripture because He knows that **only when we're planted in the soil of gratitude will we learn and grow and thrive:** "Rejoice always, pray without ceasing, give thanks in all circumstances; for this is the will of God in Christ Jesus for you."[9]

WE ARE NOT SLAVES TO OUR CIRCUMSTANCES

Have I told you about my younger daughter's struggle with dyslexia? Every day I watch Caroline wrestle with learning, with homework, with books and words. And every day it breaks my heart.

I went to a dyslexia simulation last month, where for two hours I experienced what my girl faces every hour of every day. It was exhausting.

I CHOOSE GRATITUDE

It's not just that a word shows up for someone with dyslexia with the letters out of order and written in what seems like an incomplete font—*friend* looks like *fiend* or *feirnd* or *fairnd* or *traned*—it's that those incomplete, out-of-order letters jump around while you're trying to read them, making it next to impossible to sort out what the word is. You get one word of a fifty-thousand-word book decoded and feel like a rock star. "*Friend*! It says *friend*. The word is *friend*, not *fiend*!"

Sigh. Only 49,999 words left to go.

I got home from that simulation and made a beeline for Caroline. "You are *astonishing* to me," I said.

She agonizes and wrestles and fights and cries, but she has never once given up. Yes, this is her quintessential struggle in life. But *this struggle is not who she is.*

Here's the truth Caroline reminds her full-on diagnosed-ADD mama to grab hold of: we can observe our suffering without being overtaken by our suffering. We can *see* it without becoming its slave.

Refusing to be a slave to our circumstances doesn't mean we don't fight for what's right. Scripture *commands* us to fight, in fact, by acting justly, crying out for justice, and defending the cause of the oppressed.[10] But in Christ we can fight not from a place of insecurity and outrage but from a place of reconciliation. Of calm confidence. Of peace. Of love. Why? Because our victory is sure. We've already won.

This is an important distinction, I think. You and I live in a day when true injustices are being named, brought into the light, and, on occasion, overcome and made right. I love this. God loves this. He exhorts us to bring sin into the light so that it can be rendered impotent in the world. Fighting racism, speaking out against sexual and physical abuse inside and outside the church, advocating for the welfare of children and women and minorities and immigrants and unborn children—these causes are of utmost importance to Jesus. They must be of utmost importance to us.

There are very real oppressors out there. Sometimes there are very real oppressors *in here* too, right inside the church, people victimizing others for selfish gain. I hate this reality, but we can't deny it.

Yet, despite how these situations feel to us, there is a lot we can do. For starters, we can change the language that surrounds these events. We can help those who have been victimized once and for all break free.

Even in Hollywood, advocates have taken to referring to those who have suffered at the hands of abusers as "survivors" instead of "victims," and I think it's an important shift. To define ourselves by others' wrongdoing is to render ourselves helpless and weak. To turn over our power and joy to our perpetrators only continues to bind us up.

Yes, it's tempting to find a home in our pain, to define ourselves by the awful experiences we've endured. But if I'm learning one thing from my family and friends, it's that there is an altogether better way.

My friend Tara stood up at church last night and spoke of the multiple racist statements people have made to her face throughout her life and of the outright physical attacks she's suffered and of the pain she's known year after year. Some of this inexcusable behavior occurred at a previous house of worship, which made Tara leery of reengaging in a local church. "But I decided to make a choice," she said with bravery. "I am choosing to trust again."

She went on to tell the story of joining our church and launching a series of racial reconciliation conversations that are bringing together women of various ethnicities to discuss how we truly come together and do better.

I look at Tara's impact on our congregation, and I think, *How could someone so wronged turn back to people who hurt her and say, "I want to build a bridge to get back to you. I want to try again"?*

Tara would answer my question with a single word: *Jesus.*

The way of Jesus shifts everything. In Jesus, we can acknowledge our frustration, pain, and suffering without abdicating our peace and joy. **In Jesus, we can change where we fight *from* without changing what we fight *for.*** By the power of Jesus, we can demonstrate to ourselves and others that, regardless of how grim the situation seems, God is in the business of redeeming *all* things. Out of gratitude to Jesus, we can see God's purposes in our pain.

Tara understands that while the fight she's in is real, she is assured certain victory in the end. And from that place of grateful confidence, she can reach out, she can trust, she can love.

Seeking God's Purpose Behind the Pain

Again, we can acknowledge our suffering without abdicating our joy. We can fight for justice but from a place of peace. Because we don't find our identity in a cause, we are secure in who we are in Jesus. And then there's this: when we make the brave shift from victimhood to gratitude, we affirm our understanding that *God remains committed to redeeming all things.*

Paul told the Philippians he was sure that everything that had happened to him had happened for a specific purpose. That purpose, you might guess, was to spread the gospel—God's good news of love and grace.

> I want you to know, brothers, that what has happened to me has really served to advance the gospel, so that it has become known throughout the whole imperial guard and to all the rest that my imprisonment is for Christ. And most of the brothers, having become confident in the Lord by my imprisonment, are much more bold to speak the word without fear. . . .
>
>   I will rejoice, for I know that through your prayers and the

help of the Spirit of Jesus Christ this will turn out for my deliverance, as it is my eager expectation and hope that I will not be at all ashamed, but that with full courage now as always Christ will be honored in my body, whether by life or by death. For to me to live is Christ, and to die is gain.[11]

By choosing gratitude over victimhood, Paul centered his thoughts on God's purpose behind the pain. He could focus on the impact of his imprisonment, which involved the palace guard coming to know Christ. He could see that God would always be on the move, whether in his life or through his death, whether in his peace or in his suffering. The ministry of the gospel through Paul was far from over; in fact, it was only just beginning.

But to see God's good purposes, we have to focus our gaze beyond our immediate situations. We have to remember that, even now, we have a choice: we can choose to praise and honor God right where we are, trusting that we serve a God who is both transcendent and immanent—fancy words for saying that His ways are beyond human understanding[12]—yet He chooses to be near us, to be with us, even in the hardest times when we cannot yet see how He could possibly bring anything good from our circumstances.

As I mentioned earlier, in the past five years, God's plans for me have included my dearest friend suffering both a grueling divorce and a series of massive strokes, my baby sister having her idyllic life turned upside down, my oldest child leaving for college, our family being uprooted and relocated at least in part against our wills, an eighteen-month season of such intense disillusionment that I was sure I was losing my faith or losing my mind. I absolutely agree that God's plans are benevolent and good. But perhaps I believe that only in the past tense.

In the moment, when news of the stroke comes to me, when the decision is made to relocate, when doubt threatens to take me out—do I choose to be grateful for God's plans then too?

Let me tell you about two people who have embodied this choice of gratitude over victimhood. Dee was a captain in the US Navy who was set up on a blind date. The woman's name was Roddy, and the two of them hit it off. Dee and Roddy were best friends and teammates for forty-eight years of marriage.

I met Roddy three months after Dee passed away from ALS. She graciously let me interview her during a women's ministry event, a conversation that stays with me still. "I noticed Dee was slurring his words one morning at breakfast," Roddy explained to the three hundred women sitting before her. "I knew something was amiss."

Within twelve months, a man who had been expressive and vibrant, confident and active, lay motionless, speechless, and terribly gaunt in a recumbent wheelchair at home. "Talking" involved laboriously tapping out letters with a pen held by two fingers, one slow keystroke at a time. Rolling over in bed was an impossible feat. Getting dressed on his own? That was out too. "Was I happy about this?" Roddy said. "The answer is *no*."

ALS, which stands for *amyotrophic lateral sclerosis,* is a nervous-system disease that progressively weakens muscles until there is no physical strength left at all. It's extremely rare, and it is incurable. Life expectancy from time of diagnosis is a meager two to five years. "He lived for two and a half years after we found out he had ALS," Roddy said. "And then Dee was gone."

I asked whether she'd been mad at God at any point, given the tragedy she'd endured. The concept was so foreign to her that she seemed offended I'd even ask. "Mad at God?" she said. "You know, we never once asked

'Why?' If anything, we asked 'Why *not?*'" Roddy said their faith in Jesus assured them that God would use even Dee's disease and eventual death for good.

And God has used it. And God still is using it.

At the time of Dee's diagnosis, he and Roddy had been serving in our church's marriage ministry for a decade. Even after Dee was confined to a wheelchair and incapable of vocalizing his thoughts, he showed up at ministry meetings and events, determined to keep sharing his faith, tapping out the letters on his text-to-voice simulator: *Tap, tap, tap.* "Jesus came to earth." *Tap, tap, tap.* "He died for our sins." *Tap, tap, tap.* "He rose again." *Tap, tap, tap.* "And He is seated at the right hand of the Father." *Tap, tap, tap.* "As long as I have breath"—*tap, tap, tap*—"I will tell that good news."

I looked at Roddy as she talked to our group that night, admiring her steadiness and her candor, and I realized that part of the good that God had worked together involved us, there that night. There was hardly a dry eye in the room as women absorbed the weight of Roddy's story. "I still don't fully accept that Dee is gone, never to come back," she said. "But this much I do know: his death was not an ending but an extension. And I'm determined to stick around to find out what that extension involves."

THE GIFTS WE DIDN'T ASK FOR

C. S. Lewis wrote, "My argument against God was that the universe seemed so cruel and unjust. But how had I got this idea of *just* and *unjust*? A man does not call a line crooked unless he has some idea of a straight line. What was I comparing this universe with when I called it unjust?"[13]

Maybe it's just coincidence, but here's something I've observed: the most grateful people I've known are those who have suffered the most. Now, this isn't a recommendation for us to go seek out suffering just so we can top the grateful-people chart.

But it is a plea for us to think carefully about how we respond to our boring, mundane jobs or the darkest moments of our lives. **We don't have to like our circumstances, but we can choose to look for the unexpected gifts they may bring.**

When Zac was in the depth of his depression, I remember not liking God's plans.

When I sat speechless with my sister, knowing that nothing I said would ease her pain, I remember not liking God's plans.

When Caroline cried the last night of Christmas vacation because she just couldn't muster the energy to deal with dyslexia at school the following day, I remember not liking God's plans.

When my darling friend and colleague Hannah felt leveled by so much lack in life—the lack of a boyfriend, the lack of a mentor, the lack of a friendship group, the lack of a reliable car—I didn't like God's plans at all.

When loved ones have wrestled with broken marriages and broken promises, with diagnoses and despair, with layoffs at work and lethargy in motherhood, with aging parents and angsty preteens, God's plans haven't felt especially benevolent. In those moments life feels cruel at best.

And yet.

Didn't Zac and I know God more intimately *because of* our difficulties?

Didn't Katie carve out new capacity for believing God, on her knees on those dark, dark days?

Hasn't Caroline learned to let people help her, because without help she just can't succeed?

Haven't the blessings that have come Hannah's way this past year felt sweeter than they would have if she had not felt their lack?

Don't you and I look back on the roughest of times and see that they have brought the most profound growth?

"We rejoice in our sufferings," Paul said, "knowing that suffering produces endurance, and endurance produces character, and character produces hope, and hope does not put us to shame, because God's love has been poured into our hearts through the Holy Spirit who has been given to us."[14]

Endurance and character and Spirit-enabled hope—these are marks of ones who choose gratitude.

Recently I went to throw pottery with a couple of friends for a girls' night out. Given how many potters I happen to follow on Instagram, I thought I would be an awesome potter! Surprisingly—to me, anyway—I was not. I went in with visions of creating a stunning Anthropologie-style hand-painted vase but emerged with a misshapen, muddy-hued mug.

I told one of my potter friends about this disappointment, asking why on earth she loves throwing pottery so much when it can yield such a devastating result. "That's the thing!" she said. "You work so hard and then put the piece into the fire, having no idea how it will turn out. Later, you open that kiln and hold your breath, wondering if it will have broken into a million pieces or will be the most beautiful thing you've seen."

Those really are the only two options, aren't they? Not only for pottery but also for us. When we walk through the fires we inevitably find in life, will we emerge fortified or falling apart?

Heavenly Father, help us choose wisely here. May we be found standing in our flames, praising You.

I don't have anything to offer.

I deserve some downtime.

Someone else can do it.

When is someone going to help me?

There's nowhere for me to plug in.

Run Your Race

I Choose to Seek the Good of Others

Z AC IS OUT OF TOWN, AND THIS MORNING, IN THE scramble of trying to get the kids to school, it was my turn to panic. Cooper headed toward the door with his backpack, ready for school—in his stocking feet. He just was going to walk out to the car and, I assume, into school with no shoes.

We were already late and older siblings were stressed. He has several pairs of shoes, mind you, but he couldn't find the ones he wanted to wear, which was making the whole lot of us late.

I thought, *You're making us late, Cooper. It's all your fault that your siblings are late.*

I thought, *It's selfish to make everyone else run later because you don't like the shoes that are available to wear.*

I thought, *You pick now, when Dad is out of town, to have this stand-off with me?*

And as I tumbled into a full-on emotional spiral, I opened my mouth and spoke the unthinkable. "If you are not in the car in thirty seconds with shoes on," I said, "You will get no Christmas gifts."

Gasp!

What had I just said?

Now, this declaration was flawed for several reasons. First, I knew that even if Cooper chose to wear the undesirable pair of shoes, he couldn't put them on, grab his stuff, and be in the car in half a minute.

Second, and really, the worst, I had just made an absolutely absurd threat against a kid I love, a threat I would absolutely never follow through with!

What? I was going to give presents to our three other kids and leave Cooper giftless this year?

Eventually Cooper did make it to the car with something on his feet, and eventually I drove him and the others to school. After we dropped off his siblings, my poor kid apologized for the havoc he'd wreaked and then said, "So, Mom, the coal in the stocking—does that really happen?"

Ugh.

As I've practiced the patterns we've been walking through together, I have begun to rein in my thoughts and in turn my emotions and behaviors. As this morning's implosion demonstrates, I've not done this perfectly. But there has been strong progress.

And we are headed to a level that goes one step more. We desperately want to be set free from the chaos of our minds—but set free to do what?

Our culture's idea about freedom is often that we are set free to do whatever we want. The irony is that when we go through seasons of doing whatever we want, those turn out to be our least content seasons. **We were not built to live for ourselves.**

I think of the eighteen months of doubt that held me captive and how complacency overtook my naturally zealous spirit. My spiritual doubt and disillusionment stole my energy and desire to serve. Without a bent toward service, I bent toward too much Netflix, too much social media, too much sugar, too much grief. Click, scroll, binge, cry—rinse, repeat.

And because the devil is subtle, my cravings for these things in that season kept growing and my zealous passion for souls and the things of God weakened. I had no desire to go to the grocery store, let alone go to the nations with God's message of grace.

What I experienced in that season is not at all how life was meant to be lived. You and I were made to be active, purposeful participants in God's eternal story. Complacency rewrites that script entirely.

THE ALLURE OF COMPLACENCY

Complacency is finding comfort in mediocrity, in accepting things as they are, clinging to the status quo. It's behind our tendency to check out, to zone out, to numb. If our highest aim in life is simply not rocking the boat, then why *not* eat the whole pizza, drink the whole bottle of wine, finish off the half-gallon tub of ice cream, play Candy Crush for three hours straight, or stay in bed all day?

The questions driving our thought patterns are no longer *How will God use me today?* and *How can I give Jesus to someone?* Instead, we're focused on . . .

What do I want?
What do I need?
How will I get what I want and need?
What do I feel like doing?
What will make me happier?
What will make me more comfortable?
What will make me look good?
What will make me sound smart?
What will protect me from getting hurt or from taking all the blame?

What will make me feel content?
That's the question around which all the others revolve.

I imagine few things bring the devil greater satisfaction than our comfort-seeking ways. We present no threat to him when we're wholly preoccupied with the things of this world.

As theologian and emeritus professor D. A. Carson has observed,

> People do not drift toward holiness. Apart from grace-driven effort, people do not gravitate toward godliness, prayer, obedience to Scripture, faith, and delight in the Lord. We drift toward compromise and call it tolerance; we drift toward disobedience and call it freedom; we drift toward superstition and call it faith. We cherish the indiscipline of lost self-control and call it relaxation; we slouch toward prayerlessness and delude ourselves into thinking we have escaped legalism; we slide toward godlessness and convince ourselves we have been liberated.[1]

The apostle Paul gives us the weapon of truth that frees us from the velvet-covered chains of complacency: "Set your minds on things that are above, not on things that are on earth."[2] Why? Because as those who have been buried in Christ and raised in faith, we have already died to the things of this world. Our real life is bound up with Christ.

My husband always says that the definition of *leadership* is "taking initiative for the good of others." When we reject passivity and lean into the needs around us, we see our minds set on the things of God. God is never passive. God is always working for our good and His glory.

LIE: I can do whatever I want.

TRUTH: God has set me free to serve others, not indulge myself.

You, my brothers and sisters, were called to be free. But do not use your freedom to indulge the flesh; rather, serve one another humbly in love.[3]

I CHOOSE TO SEEK THE GOOD OF OTHERS OVER MY OWN COMFORT.

THE CALL TO ACTION

I think of Jesus using the parable to tell His disciples—and, by extension, us—to "stay dressed for action and keep your lamps burning, and be like men who are waiting for their master to come home from the wedding feast, so that they may open the door to him at once when he comes and knocks."[4]

Stay dressed for action!
Keep your lamps burning!
Be waiting for your master's return!

Which I'm guessing is different from the kind of waiting you and I typically do, in hopes of the pizza guy showing up soon.

He went on—and here's my actual point: *"Blessed are those servants* whom the master finds awake when he comes. Truly, I say to you, he [the master] will dress himself for service and have them [the servants] recline at table, and he will come and serve them."[5]

See, this is why that axiom of Jesus is true, that "it is more blessed to give than to receive."[6] When we are faithful to watch for opportunities to serve, when we live our lives *at the ready* for the Master's call, we're the ones who get served in the end. Our Master will actually tend to *our* every need.

Why does it matter that we choose service instead of complacency? How does taking initiative for the good of others help us redirect our negative thoughts? What is in store for the person who serves consistently?

I Have a Choice

EMOTION
STRESS

CONSEQUENCE
EFFECTIVE

THOUGHT
I CAN DO
WHATEVER I WANT

RELATIONSHIPS
GIVING
AND LOVING

BEHAVIOR
PURSUES
SELF-INDULGENT
COMFORTS

BEHAVIOR
PURSUES THE
GOOD OF OTHERS

THOUGHT
GOD HAS SET ME FREE
TO SEEK THE GOOD
OF OTHERS OVER
MY OWN COMFORT

RELATIONSHIPS
SELF-SERVING

I CHOOSE TO SEEK
THE GOOD OF OTHERS

CONSEQUENCE
BORED

EMOTION
STRESS

Should we ever pay attention to our own problems, or are we supposed to just pretend those don't exist? What if we're tired? What if we're overwhelmed? What if we don't *feel* like doing good? Do we just fake it till we make it, or is there a more authentic path?

As followers of Christ, we have to answer these questions for ourselves, because what we believe about work might be in opposition to God's good and creative design for us.

GOD LOVES WORK

A key reason for the lover of God to choose service over complacency is that God highly values work. He *loves* work, as evidenced by His actions at the beginning of time. As we saw in our chapter on combatting cynicism, God clearly delighted in His creative efforts, treating work like the gift it is. With outright whimsy, He created those peacocks, as well as giraffes, platypuses, and more. He worked and His work was fueled by sheer delight.

Guess what? In Him, our work can be a delight too. We have been made stewards of the work God has given us. As stewards, He is our loving Master whom we trust and honor. And we work for His glory, not anyone else's.[7]

Intuitively we understand this to be true. I mean, admit it: it may feel satisfying to binge on chips and salsa while scrolling social-media feeds for an hour or two (or three?), but at *some* point don't you become as antsy and itchy as I do? Doesn't your soul start screaming for something more?

You know what our souls are saying to us? They're saying, *This just isn't cutting it for me!*

Of course it's not cutting it for you, because as long as you focus on you, it will never be enough. The fact is, **our brains are hardwired to thrive when we are serving others.** Though subconsciously we seek to be served and have our needs met, research has proven that our brains actually do much better when we're on the giving end rather than receiving end.

Serving others reduces activity in the stress- and threat-related parts of our brains.[8]

People who live with purpose sleep better and live longer.[9]

Serving others lights up a region that is part of the brain's reward system,[10] which helps us recognize and pursue things that bring us pleasure like a good meal, an encouraging interaction with a friend, or a hug from a trusted family member.

You and I were custom designed to play a role in God's eternal story and to experience deep purpose, not to while away our time with snacks and flicks. We want more than that, and there's a reason we do. God made us to crave so much more.

SURRENDER AND OBEY

It's hard to read through the Bible without clearly seeing what God expects from those who say they love Him, from those who tell Him, "I want Your will for my life."

Do you want to know God's will for your life? I'll give it to you in three words:

Surrender.
And obey.

That's it! So many books have been written on finding God's will, yet—*boom*—here it is in plain sight: "He said to them all: 'Whoever wants to be my disciple must deny themselves and take up their cross daily and follow me.'"[11]

I CHOOSE INTENTIONALITY

In our small-minded human-nature economy, we think that freedom means going our own way. In fact, freedom is found in *laying our lives down* in the service of God, the One who made us, who knows us, and who has welcomed us into fellowship with Him. It is in this state of full surrender that the longing to obey rises up in us.

Think of it: Obedience to God without full surrender is an exercise in robotically following the rules. Surrendering to God without obedience is the equivalent of faith with zero works. Which is, as James 2:17 says, *dead faith.*

No, to live out the abundance we're promised in John 10:10, we must have equal parts of both ingredients: surrender and obedience, obedience and surrender.

We go where God says to go.

We stay when God says to stay.

We lean in when God whispers our name.

We serve when He asks us to serve.

You know, we tend to glamorize Jesus's earthly ministry, as though every moment of His existence here was star studded with excitement and stimulation. Yes, there were definitely noteworthy occasions throughout those three years. A scene involving bread and fish comes to mind.

Sometimes our service gets noticed. Sometimes it's more public and people will praise us for it, like in the case of many of Jesus's miracles and healings.

But sometimes, service goes unseen. It's found in a charitable conversation, or in a shared meal. Much of Jesus's life here was spent sitting with a small group in a small room over a simple meal, talking about forgiveness and about grace, and spent noticing the hurting and serving the poor.

Nothing flashy.

Nothing "like"-able.

Nothing that would lead the evening news.

Just ordinary life with the One who was constantly bending down to meet the needs of people.

So we wipe breakfast tables and speak kindly of someone who's being criticized and write thank-you notes and build spreadsheets and take a stand against injustices and make coffee and apologize for what we said and send emails and hug a sobbing teenage daughter and change diapers and reach out to a client and teach a preschooler how to tie his shoes. We do all these things and a bajillion more—all because God prompted us to.

And as we build the spreadsheet for the glory of God, as we wipe the table in service to God and our people, we don't have quite as much time for ourselves.

It's the act of surrender.

It's the choice of obedience.

It's the joy of self-forgetfulness.

We need to become excellent at being self-forgetful.

But it's difficult to forget big things, especially ourselves.

So we shift our gaze. See, there's a greater plan for service in our lives, and this is it. We interrupt the spiral of self and the pattern of complacency when we lift our gaze off of ourselves, fix our eyes on Jesus, and run the race set before us.

What race are you running? Are you even on the track? Are you standing still? Are you gazing at your feet? Where are you in this?

But let me pull you in close and tell you that when you start taking risks for the kingdom of God and running your guts out, Satan will do everything in his power to discourage you. The devil delights in distracting us from worship, from running our races, because he knows that living out our purpose here is a direct result of our love for God, our wholehearted focus on Him. When you look at Jesus, you are so moved by His love, so moved by His grace, so moved by what He did for us, that you can't contain yourself.

So you go give Him away. It's how we're supposed to live.

SINGLE-MINDED SERVICE

Hebrews says, "Let us throw off everything that hinders and the sin that so easily entangles. And let us run with perseverance the race marked out for us, fixing our eyes on Jesus, the pioneer and perfecter of faith."[12]

I used to think that the three key elements in this passage were a linear progression: you do one, then the next, then the next. I thought I needed (first) to get rid of my sin streaks—my negative thinking patterns, my hurtful attitudes, my terribly selfish ways—so that I could (second) run my race, and then I would (third) finally see Jesus, who was probably so pleased I'd done the first two things.

But that's not at all how Jesus works, which is what told me I'd interpreted the verses wrong.

You may recall that it was when we were "still sinners," according to Romans 5:8, that "Christ died for us." We all know that if we wait until every sin that entangles us is put off, then we will never start the race! We are "being transformed into the same image from one degree of glory to another,"[13] not all at once. So, that means we can't even get rid of our sin before we run our races.

What if all this actually happens simultaneously? That would shift the importance of mission in our lives. What if we were built to run and, as we run, we fix our eyes on Jesus because we have to—we need Him!—and our sin and distraction fall away. Sin avoidance is not what Jesus died for. If we are moving, failing, finding forgiveness, and moving again, all with eyes fixed on Christ, we will desperately want to confess and deal with our sin. Because not doing that is thwarting the mission of our lives.

Do you see what a radical shift this is? As we run—as we serve others—our sin and distraction lose their hold on us, which only makes it easier to keep our eyes fixed on Christ.

Let me put it this way: if you put me on a diet and tell me that for thirty days I cannot have a cheeseburger, then guess what I'm going to think about for thirty days straight?

Cheeseburgers.

I don't even like cheeseburgers all that much. I mean, they're fine, but it's not as if I think about them all day long.

But deprive me of a cheeseburger, and *I'm going to want a cheeseburger*. Welcome to the human mind.

If we try to avoid sin by reminding ourselves day by day *not* to lie or *not* to cheat or *not* to steal or *not* to pour that third glass of wine or *not* to hide that shopping bag from our spouse or *not* to fudge that expense report at work or *not* to sneak a second serving of cheesecake after everyone else has gone to bed, then guess what we're going to focus on?

Far better to focus on what will pull us forward than try to focus on what won't push us back.

That singular thought—*I choose to serve*—leads to our taking risks on Jesus's behalf, which leads to our taking our eyes off ourselves and to seeing the needs of others for a change, which leads to our taking action to the glory of God, which leads to our depending more and more on divine strength from our Father, which leads to a deeper longing to worship Him. Those moments of unbounded worship then prompt us to long for even greater spiritual adventures, which makes us willing to take yet another risk.

That risk would lead to more service, dependency, and so on.

Now, *that's* a spiral I can get behind.

But it won't start until we choose to run.

Until we choose to serve.

Until we choose to stop prioritizing personal comfort and instead help meet others' needs.

When we serve, everything shifts. It shifts for the better—and *fast*.

I believe that single-mindedness comes as we risk for God, as we step out of our comfort zones and move into the things He's called us to. Run the race set before us. We need God, and we don't have time for our sin and our baggage and our burden because we are doing our best to follow and obey our God and do the important work that may feel insignificant on any given day.

My husband's college football coaches used to say, "You can make mistakes. Mistakes we can fix. But you'd better go at this with 110 percent. There is nothing that can happen without effort."

Friend, you and I need to be people who single-mindedly reject complacency and want God more than anything else on earth. Such surrender frees us from any worry about making mistakes or failing to look like those around us.

First Corinthians is so clear about this. If you're an elbow and you're not being an elbow in the church, the body is not well. That should bug you! In some way that should make you crazy, because you should wonder whether you're making the whole body of Christ sick.

That's what I had to come to whenever doubts crept in and suggested that maybe I was wasting my energy in ministry. This wasn't about me. My job was to obey God, and His job was to change lives.

Maybe you're one of the few who already live this way.

Maybe you're running your race and nobody's cheering, but you don't even notice because your eyes are fixed on Jesus and there are people who need you.

But more likely you've been holding back. We think we are inadequate, so we just give up and live complacent lives. No one gave us permission, so we don't do the things God called us to do. We miss getting to be part of this greater story.

Can you imagine how ineffective Jesus's ministry appeared to be, except when He did miracles? Most days He was just eating meals with sinners, telling people stories that didn't totally make sense, and ticking off the influential religious people. Then He got killed, which really looks like a ministry fail! Yet God was up to something, and Jesus knew His ultimate purpose. So He didn't care what His ministry looked like to the people around Him, and neither should we. Who are we to judge what God is up to? Who are we to judge whether it's effective for the kingdom of God?

We're talking about supernatural, eternal life change. Who are we to judge whether our token contribution is meaningful? What if we started saying, "I'm going to do whatever You say today, God! Anything. I'm in." And if every one of us did so, I'm convinced we would be blown away by the things that would start happening in our lives and in this world.

THE RACE TO THE CROSS

The next part of Hebrews 12 says, "For the joy set before him he endured the cross, scorning its shame, and sat down at the right hand of the throne of God. Consider him who endured such opposition from sinners, so that you will not grow weary and lose heart."[14]

Jesus came in human form, and He set His eyes on a joy before Him, the joy of being with us forever, reconciling people to Himself. He knew the cross was the path to joy, and He knew His life existed to save humankind. He had a big mission: save the world.

Emptying Himself was part of that mission. Being holy and perfect was part of that mission. Taking on the likeness of man was in that mission. He did all this to reveal God to us and to reveal the way that we would be saved. He didn't empty Himself just on the cross; His whole life also said, "This is how you're going to live!"

So often we go to Jesus and make Him the savior of our souls, but we don't look to Him as the model for how to live. Let me tell you what it looks like to live with this mind-set, to be single minded, to have one focus, to have the same heart, to do life well.

You become a servant. You consider others' interests above yours. Whatever God says to do, we do.

That's what Paul knew: "Do nothing from selfish ambition or conceit, but in humility count others more significant than yourselves. Let each of you look not only to his own interests, but also to the interests of others. Have this mind among yourselves, which is yours in Christ Jesus."[15]

Scripture is clear that Jesus "came not to be served but to serve, and to give his life as a ransom for many."[16] And there is no greater demonstration of this truth than Jesus humbling Himself, leaving heaven to come to earth in the form of a vulnerable baby, suffering unjust accusations, and enduring death on a Roman cross.

The race that was set before Jesus involved emptying Himself, taking on the past and present and future sin of all humankind, and spending three days in a tomb.

And yet.

You remember what Hebrews 12 makes clear: He did all these things, never once losing touch with joy. "For the joy set before him," says verse 2, "he endured the cross, scorning its shame, and sat down at the right hand of the throne of God" (NIV).

Jesus knew that His race centered on a mission that was big.

He knew that His race would take Him right to the cross.

But here is something else He knew: fulfilling the mission God had asked Him to fulfill was the best possible use of His life, so He chose it.

"For the joy set before him." That joy is real, and it is coming for us too. We have a future and a hope in Christ. **We are set free to serve so our lives will point all people to the joy we have now and the joy that is to come.**

I can't think of a better way to live.

Part Three

THINKING AS
JESUS THINKS

Who Do You Think You Are?

MY OLDEST KID WENT TO COLLEGE THIS YEAR, AND AS any dedicated mother would, I tried to cram every last lesson into his precious mind in the final weeks before he moved out. Here is the essence of my final speech, delivered to Conner there in the front seat of my car:

"Son, you are light. I know this because I have seen God in you. I have seen you go from a selfish punk kid to a young man who responds to conviction, a young man who hears from and responds to God. You love people. You put others' interests ahead of your own. All this is evidence that God is in you.

"So, you are light. It's a fact. It's your God-given nature as one of His kids.

"And you are headed into the pitch-black darkness.

"There will times when you act like the darkness, but you will never be the darkness, and you will never be at home in the darkness again."

Just as I wanted those powerful truths to take root in Conner's mind, I want the same for you and for me. Because only by clinging to those truths with all that is in us can we find moment-by-moment victory in this battle for our minds.

You see, the moment you receive Jesus, you are a new creation. But also at that point, the enemy determines to come against you. So while we are given power and authority over our minds and our lives and even the darkness coming against us, we have to fight an all-out war against sin and darkness if we don't want to be trapped by them.

Paul cast this vision for us in Philippians 3:

There are many out there taking other paths, choosing other goals, and trying to get you to go along with them. . . . They hate Christ's Cross. . . . [They] make their bellies their gods. . . . All they can think of is their appetites.

But there's far more to life for us. We're citizens of high heaven! We're waiting the arrival of the Savior, the Master, Jesus Christ, who will transform our earthy bodies into glorious bodies like his own. He'll make us beautiful and whole with the same powerful skill by which he is putting everything as it should be, under and around him.[1]

Nothing has more impact to shift our minds and lives than knowing who we are and the power and authority we have been given.

THINKING WITH THE MIND OF CHRIST

"When the fullness of time had come," Galatians 4:4–7 reminds us,

God sent forth his Son, born of woman, born under the law, to redeem those who were under the law, so that we might receive adoption as sons. And because you are sons, God has sent the

Spirit of his Son into our hearts, crying, "Abba! Father!" So
you are no longer a slave, but a son, and if a son, then an heir
through God.

We moved from being slaves to sin to being children of God. We will
probably be trying to wrap our minds around this astonishing truth until
we get to heaven.

But we must try, because it shifts everything about us. As God's children, filled with the Holy Spirit, we *have* the mind of Christ, Paul tells us
in 1 Corinthians 2:16; the issue is whether we're *using* it to think the
thoughts that Jesus might think.

Are we taking every thought captive and training our minds daily to
think like Christ?

Part 2 of this book was all about the choices we can make to help shift
our thinking from self-defeating, self-denigrating thoughts to the truth
about God and the truth about us. It was all about training our minds to
make a choice—a choice empowered by the same Spirit that led Jesus to
make the choices He made.

In other words . . .

Because Jesus stole away from the crowds to be with His Father, you
can choose to be still with God instead of distracting yourself.

Because Jesus chose to live in community with twelve men before He
ascended into heaven, you can choose to let people know you instead of
isolating yourself.

Because Jesus trusted the heavenly Father in His deepest moment of grief before He went to the cross, you can choose to stop being afraid of what the future holds and trust God.

Because Jesus had every reason to become a cynic about the world's brokenness yet constantly chose to love sinners, you can choose to delight in God and the people around you.

Because Jesus won the victory over sin and death and has made us "more than conquerors" through His love, you can choose to be grateful no matter what.[2]

Because Jesus didn't leave us alone but promised us the Holy Spirit as our helper, you can choose to get out there and do something.

Because Jesus chose these things, you and I can choose to do the same.

Despite my good grades in my high school science classes, I never loved the subject. Still, something tells me that if I went back to those biology, chemistry, and earth-science classes today, I'd love them. The more life I live, the more I crave knowing how it all works. The closer I get to God, the more fascinated I become by the intricate design of our bodies and minds.

Geek out with me for a minute over this: each thought matters.

Each thought you think matters a *lot*.

I'm not speaking arbitrarily here. I'm speaking scientifically.

Scientifically speaking, every thought we think *changes our brains.* Let me explain.

Inside your brain are about 86 billion nerve cells, called neurons.[3] If you're keeping count, that represents roughly 0.2 percent of your body's 37 trillion cells. Inside each of those 86 billion or so neurons are microtubules, each of which is thousands of times smaller in diameter than one strand of your hair. In other words, way too small to see. But their lack of visibility to the human eye doesn't make them any less important to the human experience. They mean *everything* to how we process life.

Microtubules have been called "the brains of the cell" and can be likened to a Lego set during a free build.[4] This is what I call it, anyway, when my son ditches the instructions that come with each set in favor of sitting with piles and piles of colored bricks before him, relying only on his imagination to tell him how the assembly should go.

Let's say that you're the one free-building, and you decide to assemble a tree. You might reach for several brown bricks to make the trunk and branches and then a few light and dark green bricks to fill out the leaves. Let's say that, partway through that assembly, you change your mind and want to build a fence instead. Well, you keep going with the brown bricks, but you might alter the shape of the build—from a trunk-like shape to the long slats of a fence—and you don't need the green bricks at all. If partway through *that* build, you decide that what you really want to make is a robot, then you might push aside all the brown bricks, reach for a handful of gray bricks, and take it from the top.

Inside your neurons, those microtubules are constantly building and deconstructing and reforming and coming apart and adjusting and shifting and stopping and starting again, in accordance with—wait for it!— your every thought.[5]

With each thought you think, those microtubules work hard to provide mental scaffolding to support that thought. That scaffolding gives structure to the entire nerve cell and in the truest sense alters your brain.

Mind blown yet? Wait. It gets better.

Guess how long it takes a microtubule to finish the scaffolding that gives structure to the cell? From creation to completion, what is your guess?

Ten. Minutes.

I'm not making this up.

From the time you think a thought to that thought having physiologically, scientifically, indisputably *changed your brain,* ten minutes have elapsed.[6] Your singular thought has enhanced some neural circuits and caused others to die off. It has awakened some neurons and allowed others to drift to sleep. It has built an entire microtubular city in some parts of your mind and left others a total ghost town.

All from one simple thought.

Now, there are two ways to look at this information I've just given you. One way leaves us terrified and distressed: *If I think even one negative thought, I could wreck my whole brain in ten minutes flat?*

I guess that is *technically* true. But before you spiral into despair, let's consider the other way. If you have made a habit of thinking negative thoughts, **you're only ten minutes away from a fresh start.**

Pull out the mind map you created at the beginning of this book. Would your map be the same if you mapped your thoughts today? Have you noticed the thoughts you are thinking? Have you started to interrupt them by remembering you have a choice? Are your spirals shorter and fewer?

With each positive choice made—choosing stillness instead of distraction, for example, or community instead of isolation, or surrender instead of anxiety—we are training ourselves to use the mind of Christ that we have. The more we make these positive choices, the more reflexive that approach becomes. We said that at first such a shift is *possible* through consciously, deliberately interrupting our spirals. But as we practice more, that shift becomes *probable* and then *predictable* and then utterly *instinctive* to us. Eventually we get to the place where we don't even realize we're interrupting our negative thinking in order to choose mind-of-Christ thinking, because the impulse has become so ingrained.

I liken it to cutting a road in the woods. At first the path is marked by flattened leaves on foot-worn soil. But over time the demand for that path will cause someone to come in and lay gravel on top of the dirt and then pour cement on top of that gravel and then put in mile-marker signs and streetlights at regular intervals along the way. Eventually the path is so clear cut, it would be senseless to take another route. That path is just the path you always take. That path keeps in step with God's Spirit. That path is the way of constant surrender. That path is the way of abundant humility. That path is the way of full reliance on Jesus, with every step, for every moment.

Training ourselves to take the path in our thinking is crucial because when the pressure is on and we're stressed out and hurting, how we practice is how we will play.

I recently spoke to a field full of girls at Baylor University. I still am awestruck at what went down. I preached about Paul's declaration in Romans 8:1: "There is therefore now no condemnation for those who are in Christ Jesus." Why are we living tied down and defined by our sin when the Bible tells us we are free and there is no condemnation in Jesus?

Why don't we live as if we're free? I challenged the girls to just shout out what they were struggling with and bring into light the dark hell they had been dealing with. To my surprise, one by one they started standing up. In the middle of their campus, they stood and shouted out one struggle after another.

This went on until everyone was standing. It was beautiful. I had them get in groups and pray over each thing that had kept them from being free while I asked God what He wanted to tell them next. This is when a student came up to me and said, "I think you should tell them this no longer has power over them."

I handed her the mic and said, "You tell them."

Her voice reached across the field and beyond as she shouted, "Dishonesty no longer has power over me! Dishonesty no longer has power over Baylor's campus!"

Impromptu lines began to form on each side of the stage, and students took turns shouting in the mic that their sin and their wounds no longer had power over them.

"Suicide no longer has power over me! Suicide no longer has power over Baylor's campus!"

"Pornography no longer has power over me! Pornography no longer has power over Baylor's campus!"

I have never seen anything like it! Not only were they throwing down their last 2 percent publicly; they were also denying the enemy's power over them.

God can make that kind of breakthrough happen anywhere and with anyone.

So this shame? This fear? This doubt?

It no longer has power over you!
It no longer has power over our generation!

So let's train our minds to think on that truth.

The Well-Trained Mind

I talked with an astronaut recently. He goes up into space from time to time and hangs out. My jaw was dropped for the entirety of our conversation. His normal everyday reality is *that* cool.

His name is Shane Kimbrough, and my favorite thing about him is that he is afraid of heights. Or he *used to be* afraid of heights. (Does anyone ever really get over a fear of heights? Evidently, Shane did, because the last time he was set for a space mission, he was so relaxed that he *fell asleep on the launch pad.* I'm not even kidding. His fellow astronaut people had to nudge him and say, "Hey. Shane. We're about to blast off, man.")

Shane said that his whole life is spent either preparing for a space mission, participating in a space mission, or "cooling off" from a mission, as he calls it. I asked what a mission is like, and here are some tidbits from what he said.

When you're about to launch into space, you are strapped into a capsule that is attached to rocket boosters that will blast to 17,500 miles per hour in a jiffy and get you to outer space in eight and a half minutes. You get to space and look back and see planet Earth in all her glory—the whole big round ball. You then proceed to work twelve-hour days for ten days straight, collecting samples, conducting experiments, taking walks—you know, in space. At the end of your day, you retire to soundproof sleeping quarters that are the size of a telephone booth, and you strap yourself to your bed, lest you float around all night. You peek out your window and see the oceans, the continents, the moon, the stars, before drifting off to sleep.

Now, not only is it hard on an astronaut's body to be in space (on average, astronauts lose about 1 percent of their bone mass per month spent in space), but it's also hard on their minds. They are separated from friends and family and normal earthly routines for days—sometimes months—on end. Despite the wonderful aspects of their job, they know that life is going on without them back home. They can feel isolated. Emotions can run dark.

Shane told me about an extended mission he was on last year, when he really had to mind his mind. "We launched in September and were scheduled to be home mid-February. In late January, our crew received some troubling news from mission control. For a whole host of reasons, we wouldn't be landing until April now."

This wasn't like being an hour later for dinner; Shane would be *two months* late.

Shane was ready to be home. Shane's wife and kids were ready for him to be home. The entire crew ached to get home. Yet they would not be going home.

"How in the world did you cope?" I asked him, and in response he said four words I'll never, ever forget.

"I trusted my training."

Shane *so believed* in his work, in his mission to serve humanity, in the fact that mission control had his best interests at heart, in God's faithful provision, come what may, that he was able to arrest the thoughts that would have otherwise derailed him and think on more useful things.

"I spent years and years learning how to be a successful astronaut," he said. "I believed the best, I called my wife, and I got busy finishing my task."

"I trusted my training," Shane told me, words that lingered with me for days.

It's not easy to stop believing lies. We can't simply sit back and wait for our minds to heal, for our thoughts to change. We train. That's how truth gains the victory in the battle for our minds.

We stick our heads in our Bibles day in and day out. You might not be able to fully grab hold of truth on day 2, but on day 102, it will be taking hold in your heart and mind.

We wake up in the morning, and rather than get on our phones, we get on our knees and we submit our thoughts to Jesus.

We invest in healthy relationships and intentionally go to them when we start to spiral.

We choose well. Daily. Moment by moment. We train our minds. And when a new temptation to spiral presents itself, we trust our training.

Think of Who You Really Are

Kate, my sixteen-year-old daughter, looked up from her sushi and said, "Mom, my mind is spinning! I know the right answers, but I need you to remind me: Who does Jesus say that I am?"

I could see it. She felt desperate. She felt alone. Her mind had been running wild for some time, and she couldn't make it stop. She needed me to reach in, help grab the reins, and slow it down.

I was so struck by this amazing young woman in front of me that I kind of reverted to seeing her as my little girl, now all grown up, instead of as a fierce woman about to change the world. "You are smart!" I said. "You are passionate. And generous and creative and cute—"

"Mom," Kate interrupted. "I don't want to know what *you* say about me. I want to know what *Jesus* says."

Oh yeah. Right. Of course.

Because everything else is like chasing the wind, Ecclesiastes says.[7]

Our minds spin and spin, often grabbing hold of lies in the search for stability. Messages get mixed, and it feels as if we can't quite put our feet back down on the simple truths of what it means to love Jesus, what it means to be loved by Jesus.

If, like Kate, you need to be reminded of who Jesus says you are, may

I put my hands on the sides of your face and tell you again what He says about Himself and about you?

I AM WHO I AM. *Exodus 3:14*

I am the beginning and the end.
I am the first, and I am the last. *Revelation 22:13*

I am light; in me there is no darkness at all. *1 John 1:5*

My hand laid the foundation of the earth,
  and my right hand spread out the heavens;
when I call to them,
  they stand forth together. *Isaiah 48:13*

Before I formed you in the womb I knew you. *Jeremiah 1:5*

I chose you and appointed you that you should go and bear fruit and that your fruit should abide, so that whatever you ask the Father in my name, he may give it to you. *John 15:16*

I am he who blots out your transgressions.
I will not remember your sins. *Isaiah 43:25*

To all who receive Me,
who believe in My name,
I give the right to become children of God. *John 1:12*

Do you not know that you are God's temple
and that God's Spirit dwells in you? *1 Corinthians 3:16*

My Spirit is within you. *Ezekiel 36:27*

I will not leave you. *Deuteronomy 31:8*

I will equip you for every good work I've planned. *Hebrews 13:21*

I gave you a spirit not of fear
but of power and love and self-control. *2 Timothy 1:7*

I will build my church through you,
and the gates of hell will not overcome it. *Matthew 16:18*

I will comfort you as you wait. *Isaiah 66:13*

I will remind you this is all real. *John 14:26*

I am on my way. *Revelation 3:11*

My steadfast love endures forever. *Psalm 138:8*

In just a little while . . .
I am coming and I will take you to the place where I am.
Hebrews 10:37; John 14:3

You will inherit the earth. *Psalm 25:13*

You will be with Me.
I will wipe every tear from your eyes, and death will be no more.
Behold, I am making all things new. *Revelation 21:3–5*

My kingdom is coming.
My will will be done on earth as it is in heaven. *Matthew 6:10*

God has declared these truths about Himself and about me. All these things are true for you and for anyone who loves and follows Jesus. This is who we are because of whose we are. We make our choices based on these truths. And our God doesn't change and always delivers on His promises.

Dangerous Thinking

TODAY AS I REALIZED HOW CLOSE I WAS TO FINISHING this book, I rallied a dozen people who love me to pray. I may never have met you, yet I care deeply about your freedom. I hope you can read that motivation in my words. I care deeply, yet I recognize that the freedom I'm referring to comes only by a work of God, by His Spirit, by His divine intervention in your life.

Separate from that prayer rally, my friend Jess, who has no idea what I'm up to today, just sent me a text. She doesn't know that I'm working on a chapter just now about how *contagious* our minds are and about how, when we're conformed to the mind of Christ, we can influence everyone around us for powerful, almost indescribable good. She doesn't know the prayers being prayed, that you'd be set *totally free.*

Attached to her text is a picture of her dad. He is a godly man, a great dad, a faithful husband. He also is a man with a substance abuse problem.

He finished a season in rehab a few months ago, and boy, did he return to his church and community on a *mission.* After his program finished, he went back and began leading Bible studies at the rehab facility he'd just left.

The picture Jess texted me was of six men, all of different ages, ethnicities, and interests. They were all smiles, seated around a dinner table.

Jess wrote, "My dad woke up Saturday morning with the idea to invite his rehab buddies over for dinner, so he and my mom made the invite, and a few hours later they all showed up. My family is still fragile, but these are the things that help me see that God really does bring beauty from ashes."

Only God can take our most broken parts and turn them into thumbs-up moments of hope around grilled hamburgers and potato salad. Only God can take the thing we want to hide and build the greatest story we will ever tell. Only God can turn people we might have looked down on into friends and colaborers and brothers in Him.

Only God.

Our Singular Focus

Aside from the apostle Paul and Jesus, Peter might just be my favorite person in the Bible. My love for him runs deep for two simple reasons: first, he was a radical, a renegade, a guy living hair-on-fire for the Lord, and I like to think that I have a little of that Jesus-freak passion running through my veins. Second, Peter is perhaps best known for the unbelievable mistakes he made—a reality to which I can relate. He was a little . . . overconfident. A certain incident comes to mind when he told Jesus in Matthew 26, in essence, "What do You mean I'll deny You? That's preposterous."

This was, of course, right before Peter denied Jesus, not once or twice but three times.

So, there's that.

But in other places in Scripture, Peter was this passionate, devoted, faithful disciple, one in whom Jesus could place His trust.

Acts 2 reminds us that it was Peter on the Day of Pentecost who stood before the masses and shared the truth, prompting thousands to follow Christ, which is when the church was birthed.

But the scene that knits my heart closest to Peter's heart is recorded in Matthew 14. Immediately following the feeding of the five thousand, during which Jesus somehow multiplied a boy's sack lunch to feed a hungry horde of people, we read that Jesus "made the disciples get into the boat and go before him to the other side, while he dismissed the crowds."[1] Here's what happened next:

> After he had dismissed the crowds, he went up on the mountain by himself to pray. When evening came, he was there alone, but the boat by this time was a long way from the land, beaten by the waves, for the wind was against them. And in the fourth watch of the night he came to them, walking on the sea. But when the disciples saw him walking on the sea, they were terrified, and said, "It is a ghost!" and they cried out in fear. But immediately Jesus spoke to them, saying, "Take heart; it is I. Do not be afraid."
>
> And Peter answered him, "Lord, if it is you, command me to come to you on the water." He said, "Come." So Peter got out of the boat and walked on the water and came to Jesus. But when he saw the wind, he was afraid, and beginning to sink he cried out, "Lord, save me." Jesus immediately reached out his hand and took hold of him, saying to him, "O you of little faith, why did you doubt?" And when they got into the boat, the wind ceased. And those in the boat worshiped him, saying, "Truly you are the Son of God."[2]

That picture of Peter with singular focus on the face of Christ, babystepping over those cresting whitecaps—I can't quit thinking about it. That scene is what inspired part 2 of this book, in fact—this idea that regardless of the wind and the rain and the uncertainty and the fear, when our eyes are fixed on Jesus, we travel *on top of,* not under, those waves.

When we shift from the thoughts that distract and choose to fix our thoughts single-mindedly on Him, everything shifts!

But it wasn't Peter's strength or willpower that kept him afloat; it was the object of his gaze: Jesus's face.

The enemy is trying to disrupt our single-mindedness. Winning is focusing on Christ. If we think on Christ, if we zoom in and are consumed with Him, then everything else grows strangely dim. But the enemy wants you to focus on anything but Jesus.

Because we get really dangerous when we get single minded. Peter did. Peter would flail a bit between that lesson on the water and Jesus's ascension, but a time would come when his life would snap into complete focus. His spirals of self-importance and anxiety would lessen, and he aimed himself fully toward his mission.

And when that happened, the church was launched into existence, thousands and thousands were saved and began to follow Jesus, countries were evangelized, and generations were changed forever.

I know you might be thinking, *Jennie, that's great. But I just need to quit feeling so anxious.* I know. But part of quitting feeling anxious is finding an altogether different reason to live. When Christ is our prize and heaven is our home, we get less anxious because we know our mission, our hope, our God cannot be taken from us.

A NEW WAY TO THINK

You know, this is what this entire book comes down to: our thoughts being wholly consumed by the mind of Christ. This matters because, as we looked at earlier, our thoughts dictate our beliefs, which dictate our actions, which form our habits, which compose the sum of our lives. As we think, so we live. When we think on Christ, we live on the foundation of Christ, our gaze fixed immovably on Him. Wind? What wind? Waves? What waves? We step. We walk. We *make it across that sea.* Prison? Well, okay. At least the guards might be saved. Shipwreck? Hmmm, okay. Apparently God wants me here instead of there, where the ship was headed.

A whole new way to think—that's what we're after here.

It's been more than a year since I experienced that season of unwelcome 3 a.m. wake-up calls. And while I still do wake in the middle of the night every so often, the interruption no longer fills me with terror and dread. Far from it! During those early-morning times, I now experience something like *peace*. In fact, in a truly redemptive turn of events, God took the most upsetting and disruptive part of my daily experience and began to use it for good. It's no exaggeration to say that the bulk of this book was written between the hours of 3 and 5 a.m., morning by morning, week by week, month by month. Sleeplessness gave way to sacredness. Isn't that a beautiful thing?

In the dark, my mind used to spiral, afraid that there was no good place to land. Afraid that God was not real.

Afraid that I was not safe.

Afraid that I was not seen.

Afraid of the days to come.

Those fears, I would learn, were frauds. I *was* seen. I *was* safe. God *was* real.

God remains so real today.

Even now as I type from my bed, my husband asleep beside me, my computer screen aglow, and my fingers moving too slowly for my rapid-fire thoughts, I am at home. At home with God again. He chose me. He chose me and set me apart. I am not alone in the dark.

I am known.

I am chosen.

I am safe.

I am God's, and He is mine.

So again and again in the night, I make my choice. I choose to talk to God instead of doubt Him. I choose to be grateful for all He has done. I choose to obey Him, no matter how I feel.

This is my upward spiral. I am at peace. And I so desperately want this for you. I want you to live free and give Jesus away to others.

You Can Help Turn the Tide

I got home one afternoon to find Kate standing in the kitchen with another girl. "Mom," she said, "this is Rachel. She met Jesus a few weeks ago and has never owned a Bible. I'm going to show her a few things in mine."

The girls headed off to Kate's bedroom, and an hour or so later, I heard them sorting out the difference between the Old and the New Testaments, between the Gospels and the Epistles, between the Major and the Minor Prophets. I thought about all the things my kid could have been doing that afternoon, and I thanked God that she was doing this. In Psalm 3:3, the psalmist said that God is "the lifter of my head," and that imagery is exactly what came to mind as I saw Rachel engaging with Kate. I didn't know Rachel's background or story, the specific struggles she'd been made to endure. But there on that bed, a Bible in her lap, I saw her eyes filled with a new hope.

I listened to an audiobook recently about the power of our minds, and the author had this to say:

When you choose not to think that negative thought, and you replace it with a positive one instead, you aren't just shifting your own reality. You're shifting reality for the whole human species. You're adding to the sum of kindness and compassion in the world. You're reinforcing that new reality field. . . . You're helping transform it into an irresistible force that turns the tide of history.[3]

In other words, we all have contagious minds.

Being consumed by the mind of Jesus cannot stop with us. This is my prayer for all of us. If thousands of people read this book and start to shift, this way of thinking can become contagious—and we could see a generation freed.

I believe it is possible. I pray it will be so.

Press on, sweet friend. "Do not be conformed to this world, but be transformed by the renewal of your mind, that . . . you may discern what is the will of God."[4]

Why? Why would that matter so much—to discern the will of God? Because He isn't just after your freedom. He prepared good works in advance for you so that a whole lot of other people could be set free.[5]

When we take every thought captive and reclaim our thinking patterns from the lies of the enemy, we are set free to set others free. May we steward our freedom well.

God, I pray that You would set this reader free. God, in Your power would You help us fight the enemy hell-bent on destroying us and help us remember that the power to choose a different way is ours in You?

And then help us give that away to a world aching for a new way to think and live.

In Jesus's name, amen.

Acknowledgments

I've written a few books, and this by a million miles was the most difficult. Maybe it's because of the war I had to personally fight not just to write this book but to live this book. Or maybe it's because this matters so much and hell was against it. But no matter the reason, I couldn't have made it through this process without the small army God has placed in my life not only to help me do what He's called me to do but, more important, to help me live how He's called me to live.

First up is God. You fought for me when nothing but You could have saved me. Thank You for setting me free not just from my sin but from the toxic ways I'd become stuck and barely noticed. I'll never get over the great saving blood of Jesus Christ and that You would save a wretch like me.

Zac, you are the best teammate I could ever dream of, and none of this would exist without you: from sending me on writing retreats while you covered car pool and homework and meals, to comforting me in all my doubts and fears, to believing in this mission God has placed on our lives. As you always say, you'll get all the credit in heaven. We all know it's true.

To my kids, Conner, Kate, Caroline, and Cooper, who seem to never resent this costly calling. In fact, not only do you not resent it; you celebrate and champion everything I do. I've watched God grow you from people who need me to people who challenge me daily. You're some of my favorite people on earth, so bonus that I get to be your mom.

Chloe Hamaker, you believe in me more than I believe in myself. This isn't a job to you; it's a calling. So I guess I need to thank God for calling you because He knew I could not do ministry without you. You are my Aaron holding up my arms as I do this scary mission. Your fingerprints are all over this book. Thank you for helping me shape it into something helpful, usually in the middle of the night.

Lysa TerKeurst, you and your team helped me believe in the message of this book! I walked out of your offices that day focused and certain God could use this book to help people. Thanks for taking time with us.

Ashley Wiersma, I was scared to allow someone into the writing process with me. But I knew in every other part of my life, team makes us better. I knew being alone with my thoughts and computer wasn't the best way to produce this book. Thank you for making me a better writer and for patiently watching as God built the thing He wanted to exist here.

Laura Barker, I always say you should be on the cover of my books as a coauthor, because that's how serious your editing is. It's always painful when we're in the middle of it, but you make me a better writer, and you made this book clearer and stronger. Obviously, this is not simply a job to you. You are so passionate, and I'm honored to have worked with you on this project.

Curtis, Karen, and Yates & Yates, you aren't primarily my agent; you are our friends. Zac and I trust you and appreciate you more and more every year. You saw the hand of God on my life when barely anyone else did. You believed in me and threw in completely, and I'll never get over God's provision in giving me a team like you.

Caroline Parker, you held together some of the most important parts of our lives so this book could exist. Thank you for endlessly serving our family and making us more sane. Thank you for transcribing a lot of my words so I didn't have to start this book from scratch and for researching and talking through so many of these ideas with me. You make life and work more fun!

IF:Gathering team (Brooke, Jordyn, Amy, Lisa, Aly, Kali, Katy, Traci, Hannah M., Kristen, Kayley, Caroline, Morgan, Hannah R., and others), you helped me live this out and cheered me on and prayed for me while I was away writing. Thank you for letting me constantly work out these truths among you. Thank you for forgiving me and allowing me to be an imperfect leader. And for keeping IF:Gathering up and running while I was drowning in writing.

To my home church, Watermark, thank you for allowing me to teach this on the ground with you. I learned so much as we dug into Paul and his words and life. Without those six weeks together, this book wouldn't exist. But I also know that without the community and teaching and accountability I receive here, I could never do what I do. Thank you for supporting me in so many ways.

I'm blessed to have dear friends and family who get what I do and support it. Coach and Nana, Mom and Dad, Ashley and Pete, Brooke and Tony, Katie and Aaron, living life in the context of healthy family has meant the most. I'm so grateful for such a God-fearing and supportive family. To my small group and extended friends, new and old, you are fierce and fun and make ministry and life worth it to me. Thanks for not quitting me.

WaterBrook team (Tina, Campbell, Laura B., Ginia, Johanna, Bev, Lori, Mark, Laura W., and Kelly), you have believed in me since day one and have worked to spread this message far and wide. You are passionate people who obviously work for the glory of God and the good of people. I don't take for granted a seat at your table. Thank you for offering me one and dreaming big things for this work.

Notes

Chapter 1
1. 2 Corinthians 10:5.
2. Romans 12:1–2.
3. Aditi Nerurkar et al., "When Physicians Counsel About Stress: Results of a National Study," *JAMA Internal Medicine* 173, no. 1 (January 14, 2013): 76, https://jamanetwork.com/journals/jamainternalmedicine/fullarticle/1392494.
4. Dr. Caroline Leaf, *Switch On Your Brain: The Key to Peak Happiness, Thinking, and Health* (Grand Rapids, MI: Baker, 2015), 33.
5. Romans 12:2.
6. John Owen, *On Temptation and the Mortification of Sin in Believers* (Philadelphia: Presbyterian Board of Publication), 154.
7. Dr. Caroline Leaf, *Switch on Your Brain Every Day: 365 Readings for Peak Happiness, Thinking, and Health* (Grand Rapids, MI: Baker, 2018), back cover.

Chapter 2
1. Ephesians 1:4–5.
2. A. W. Tozer, *The Pursuit of God* (Camp Hill, PA: Christian Publications, 1982), 103.

Chapter 3
1. Beth Moore, *Get Out of That Pit: Straight Talk About God's Deliverance* (Nashville: Thomas Nelson, 2007), 23, 49, 71.

Chapter 4
1. Psalm 139:7–10.
2. Psalm 139:1–2.

3. Psalm 139:5.

4. Acts 9:17–18.

5. 1 Corinthians 2:14, 16.

6. "Mental Health Conditions," National Alliance on Mental Illness, www.nami.org/Learn-More/Mental-Health-Conditions.

7. Emphasis added.

Chapter 5

1. Romans 8:11.

2. 2 Corinthians 10:3–6.

3. 2 Corinthians 10:5–6, MSG.

4. 2 Corinthians 5:17.

5. Daniel J. Siegel, *Mind: A Journey to the Heart of Being Human* (New York: W. W. Norton, 2017), 179, 185, 266, www.psychalive.org/dr-daniel-siegel-neuroplasticity.

6. Romans 7:22–23.

7. Romans 8:6–11.

8. Isaiah 26:3, NLT.

Chapter 6

1. Raj Raghunathan, "How Negative Is Your 'Mental Chatter'?," *Psychology Today,* October 10, 2013, www.psychologytoday.com/us/blog/sapient-nature/201310/how-negative-is-your-mental-chatter.

2. John 16:33, NIV.

3. 2 Peter 1:3.

4. 2 Corinthians 10:6 (MSG).

5. Mind mapping was popularized by Tony Buzan, and the application here is adapted from Shainna Ali, "Mind Mapping: A Guide to Achieving Your Goals in 2018," ACA Member Blogs, American Counseling Association, December 6, 2017, www.counseling.org/news/aca-blogs/aca-member-blogs/aca-member-blogs/2017/12/06/mind-mapping-a-guide-to-achieving-your-goals-in-2018.

6. Matthew 6:33.
7. Matthew 22:37–39.

Chapter 7

1. Genesis 3:6, NIV.
2. 2 Samuel 11:2.
3. Luke 1:38.
4. Luke 22:42.
5. Proverbs 23:7, NKJV.
6. Ephesians 6:12.
7. Romans 8:5–6.
8. 2 Corinthians 11:14.
9. James 1:14–15; John 10:10.
10. Deuteronomy 20:3–4.

Chapter 8

1. Psalm 46:10.
2. Psalm 139:2, NCV.
3. Galatians 6:7–9.
4. Romans 2:4.
5. Psalm 84:10, NIV.
6. James 4:4–7.
7. James 4:8.
8. Barbara Bradley Hagerty, "Prayer May Reshape Your Brain . . . and Your Reality," NPR, May 20, 2009, www.npr.org/templates/story /story.php?storyId=104310443.
9. Sam Black, *The Porn Circuit: Understand Your Brain and Break Porn Habits in 90 Days* (Owosso, MI: Covenant Eyes, 2019), 38, www.covenanteyes.com/resources/heres-your-copy-of-the-porn -circuit.
10. Cary Barbor, "The Science of Meditation," *Psychology Today,* May 1, 2001, www.psychologytoday.com/us/articles/200105/the-science -meditation.

11. Alice G. Walton, "7 Ways Meditation Can Actually Change the Brain," *Forbes,* February 9, 2015, www.forbes.com/sites/aliceg walton/2015/02/09/7-ways-meditation-can-actually-change-the -brain/#98deead14658.

12. Walton, "7 Ways."

13. Charles F. Stanley, "How to Meditate on Scripture," In Touch Ministries, August 3, 2015, www.intouch.org/Read/Blog/how-to -meditate-on-scripture.

14. Matthew 11:28–30.

15. Galatians 5:16–26.

16. For more on cognitive reframing, see Elizabeth Scott, "4 Steps to Shift Perspective and Change Everything," Verywell Mind, June 28, 2019, www.verywellmind.com/cognitive-reframing-for-stress -management-3144872.

17. Poem by Rachel Landingham. Gratefully acknowledged and used by permission.

Chapter 9

1. Larry Crabb, *SoulTalk: The Language God Longs for Us to Speak* (Brentwood, TN: Integrity, 2003), 138.

2. Romans 12:10; Romans 12:16; 2 Corinthians 13:11; Galatians 5:13; Ephesians 4:32.

3. 1 John 1:7.

4. Matthew D. Lieberman, *Social: Why Our Brains Are Wired to Connect* (New York: Crown, 2013), 9.

5. Liz Miller, "Interpersonal Neurobiology: What Your Relation-ships Mean to Your Brain," Liz Miller Counseling, https:// lizmillercounseling.com/2017/08/interpersonal-neurobiology -relationships.

6. Amy Banks, "Humans Are Hardwired for Connection? Neurobiol-ogy 101 for Parents, Educators, Practitioners and the General Public," interview, Wellesley Centers for Women, September 15, 2010, www.wcwonline.org/2010/humans-are-hardwired-for

-connection-neurobiology-101-for-parents-educators-practitioners
-and-the-general-public.

7. "The Science of Love: See How Social Isolation and Loneliness Can
Impact Our Health," Living Love Mindfulness Medicine, February
21, 2017, https://livinglovecommunity.com/2017/02/21/science
-love-see-social-isolation-loneliness-can-impact-health.

8. Philippians 2:1–2.

9. Colossians 3:12–16.

10. Amy Paturel, "Power in Numbers: Research Is Pinpointing the
Factors That Make Group Therapy Successful," *Monitor on Psychology,* November 2012, www.apa.org/monitor/2012/11/power.

11. Shelley E. Taylor et al., "Biobehavioral Responses to Stress in
Females: Tend-and-Befriend, Not Fight-or-Flight," *Psychological
Review* 107, no. 3 (2000): 418; Concordia University, "Poor Social
Integration = Poor Health," *EurekAlert!,* January 20, 2015, www
.eurekalert.org/pub_releases/2015-01/cu-psi012015.php.

12. Brené Brown, *Daring Greatly: How the Courage to Be Vulnerable
Transforms the Way We Live, Love, Parent, and Lead* (New York:
Avery, 2012), 12.

13. Ephesians 5:13–14.

14. Psalm 32:3; Proverbs 28:13.

15. 1 Corinthians 11:1, NIV.

16. Ecclesiastes 4:9–12.

17. Luke 6:31.

18. James 5:16.

Chapter 10

1. Matthew 6:25–34.

2. Romans 5:5.

3. Ephesians 3:16.

4. Tim Newman, "Anxiety in the West: Is It on the Rise?," Medical
News Today, September 5, 2018, www.medicalnewstoday.com
/articles/322877.php.

5. Luke 12:7, NLT.
6. Philippians 4:6–8, NIV.
7. Don Joseph Goewey, "85% of What We Worry About Never Happens," Don Joseph Goewey, December 7, 2015, https://don josephgoewey.com/eighty-five-percent-of-worries-never-happen-2, citing data summarized in Robert L. Leahy, *The Worry Cure: Seven Steps to Stop Worry from Stopping You* (New York: Three Rivers, 2005), 18–19.
8. John 8:42–44.
9. Philippians 1:21–22, NIV.
10. 2 Corinthians 12:9, NIV.
11. 1 Corinthians 10:13.
12. Hebrews 13:5–6.
13. Psalm 54:4.
14. Psalm 139:1–2.
15. 2 Peter 1:3.
16. 1 John 3:1–2.
17. Galatians 1:10.
18. 2 Corinthians 12:9–11.
19. James 1:17, NIV.
20. Corrie ten Boom, *The Hiding Place* (New York: Bantam Books, 1974), 29.
21. 1 Peter 5:7.
22. Luke 12:27–28.

Chapter 11

1. Brené Brown, *Daring Greatly: How the Courage to Be Vulnerable Transforms the Way We Live, Love, Parent, and Lead* (New York: Avery, 2015), 124.
2. Paul K. Piff et al., "Awe, the Small Self, and Prosocial Behavior," *Journal of Personality and Social Psychology* 108, no. 6 (2015): 883, www.apa.org/pubs/journals/releases/psp-pspi0000018 .pdf.

3. 2 Corinthians 3:16–18, MSG.

4. Romans 8:28, NIV.

5. *Oxford English Dictionary Online,* s.v. "cynic," www.oed.com.

6. Philippians 4:4–9.

7. Clyde Kilby, quoted in John Piper, *Taste and See: Savoring the Supremacy of God in All of Life* (Colorado Springs: Multnomah, 2005), 70.

8. If you haven't seen this footage, watch it. You'll be glad you did. "Hurricane Harvey: Man Plays Piano in Flooded Texas Home," BBC, August 31, 2017, www.bbc.com/news/av/world-us-canada -41118462/hurricane-harvey-man-plays-piano-in-flooded-texas -home.

9. Psalm 19:1.

10. Emily Perl Kingsley, "Welcome to Holland," National Down Syndrome Society, 1987, www.ndss.org/resources/a-parents -perspective.

11. Michiel van Elk et al., "The Neural Correlates of the Awe Experience: Reduced Default Mode Network Activity During Feelings of Awe," *Human Brain Mapping,* August 15, 2019, https://pure.uva.nl /ws/files/37286954/Elk_et_al_2019_Human_Brain_Mapping.pdf.

12. Bruno Mars, "Grenade," by Bruno Mars et al., *Doo-Wops & Hooligans,* copyright © 2010, Elektra Entertainment Group.

Chapter 12

1. Romans 12:3, 10, NIV.

2. Andrew Murray, *Humility: The Beauty of Holiness,* 2nd ed. (London: James Nisbet, 1896), 7, 12, 13, 14, 68, 95.

3. Murray, *Humility,* 47.

4. Genesis 3:5.

5. Philippians 2:5–8, NIV.

6. Carrie Steckl, "Are Compassion and Pride Mutually Exclusive?" American Addiction Centers Inc., www.mentalhelp.net/blogs/are -compassion-and-pride-mutually-exclusive.

7. Philippians 3:7–11.

8. Matthew 16:24; 1 Peter 4:13; Ephesians 4:1–3, NIV.

9. Philippians 2:5, NIV.

10. Philippians 2:6–8.

11. Psalm 25:8–9; Proverbs 11:2; Proverbs 22:4; Matthew 6:3–4.

12. 2 Corinthians 12:9.

13. John B. Evans, quoted in Harriet Rubin, "Success and Excess," *Fast Company*, September 30, 1998, www.fastcompany.com/35583 /success-and-excess.

14. Murray, *Humility*, 47.

15. Charles Haddon Spurgeon, "Working Out What Is Worked In" (sermon, Metropolitan Tabernacle, London, July 12, 1868), Spurgeon Center, www.spurgeon.org/resource-library/sermons/working -out-what-is-worked-in#flipbook.

16. *Tyndale Bible Dictionary*, s.v. "humility," ed. Walter A. Elwell and Philip W. Comfort (Wheaton, IL: Tyndale, 2001), 618.

17. John 3:30.

18. Murray, *Humility*, 81.

Chapter 13

1. Philippians 1:3–6.

2. Isaiah 41:10.

3. Alex Korb, "The Grateful Brain: The Neuroscience of Giving Thanks," *Psychology Today*, November 20, 2012, www.psychology today.com/us/blog/prefrontal-nudity/201211/the-grateful-brain.

4. Korb, "Grateful Brain."

5. Amy Morin, "7 Scientifically Proven Benefits of Gratitude," *Psychology Today*, April 3, 2015, www.psychologytoday.com/us/blog/what -mentally-strong-people-dont-do/201504/7-scientifically-proven -benefits-gratitude.

6. 1 Thessalonians 5:16–18.

7. Acts 9:23, 29; 13:50; 14:5, 19; 15:5, 39; 16:22–23, 39; 17:5–7, 13–14, 18; 21:27–30; 22:24–25; 23:33–27:2; 27:41–28:1; 28:3–5, 14–16.

8. 2 Corinthians 11:24–26; Galatians 2:11–14; 2 Timothy 1:15; 4:10.

9. 1 Thessalonians 5:16–18.

10. Micah 6:8; Luke 18:7; Proverbs 31:9.

11. Philippians 1:12–14, 18–21.

12. Isaiah 55:9.

13. C. S. Lewis, *Mere Christianity* (New York: HarperOne, 2001), 38.

14. Romans 5:3–5.

Chapter 14

1. D. A. Carson, *For the Love of God: A Daily Companion for Discovering the Riches of God's Word,* vol. 2 (Wheaton, IL: Crossway Books, 1999), "January 23."

2. Colossians 3:2.

3. Galatians 5:13, NIV.

4. Luke 12:35–36.

5. Luke 12:37, emphasis added.

6. Acts 20:35.

7. Genesis 1:28; Matthew 25:14–30; Colossians 3:23–24.

8. Christopher Bergland, "3 Specific Ways That Helping Others Benefits Your Brain," *Psychology Today,* February 21, 2016, www.psychologytoday.com/us/blog/the-athletes-way/201602/3-specific-ways-helping-others-benefits-your-brain.

9. Janice Wood, "Having a Purpose in Life Linked to Better Sleep," *Psych Central,* August 8, 2018, https://psychcentral.com/news/2017/07/09/having-a-purpose-in-life-linked-to-better-sleep/122940.html; Kashmira Gander, "People with a Sense of Purpose Live Longer, Study Suggests," *Newsweek,* May 24, 2019, https://www.newsweek.com/people-sense-purpose-live-longer-study-suggests-1433771.

10. Bergland, "3 Specific Ways."

11. Luke 9:23, NIV.

12. Hebrews 12:1–2, NIV.

13. 2 Corinthians 3:18.

14. Hebrews 12:2–3, NIV.

15. Philippians 2:3–5.

16. Mark 10:45.

Chapter 15

1. Philippians 3:18–21, MSG.

2. Romans 8:37.

3. James Randerson, "How Many Neurons Make a Human Brain? Billions Fewer Than We Thought," *Guardian,* February 28, 2012, www.theguardian.com/science/blog/2012/feb/28/how-many -neurons-human-brain.

4. Jon Lieff, "Are Microtubules the Brain of the Neuron," Searching for the Mind, November 29, 2015, http://jonlieffmd.com/blog/are -microtubules-the-brain-of-the-neuron.

5. Lieff, "Are Microtubules."

6. John McCrone, quoted in Dawson Church, *The Genie in Your Genes: Epigenetic Medicine and the New Biology of Intention* (Santa Rosa, CA: Elite Books, 2007), 141.

7. Ecclesiastes 1:14, NIV.

Chapter 16

1. Matthew 14:22.

2. Matthew 14:23–33.

3. Dawson Church, *Mind to Matter: The Astonishing Science of How Your Brain Creates Material Reality* (Carlsbad, CA: Hay, 2018), Kindle edition, chap. 7.

4. Romans 12:2.

5. Ephesians 2:10.

NO MORE PRETENDING.
NO MORE PERFORMING.
NO MORE FIGHTING
TO PROVE YOURSELF.

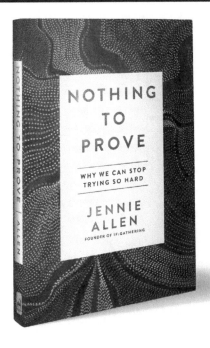

Jesus didn't save you so you could try harder. So you could fear more. So you could struggle to be enough. He came that you might have life and have it abundantly. In *Nothing to Prove*, Jennie Allen offers us the freedom to rest in the grace of God's enough-ness.

WATERBROOK

Listen to Jennie's Podcast

made
for this
with jennie allen

iTunes | Google Play | Spotify | Stitcher

IF:GATHERING

IF:Gathering exists to equip women with
gospel-centered resources, events, and community
so that they may learn about who God is and disciple
other women right where they are.

WANT TO LEARN MORE?

Sign up for our email list at ifgathering.com.